SECRETS OF THE SIX-FIGURE AUTHOR

MASTERING THE INNER GAME OF WRITING, PUBLISHING AND MAR

TOM C

D0861845

Published by TCK Publishing

www.TCKPublishing.com

Get the free Kindle publishing and marketing video training series at:

www.EbookPublishingSchool.com

EARNINGS DISCLAIMER

When addressing financial matters in any of books, sites, videos, newsletters or other content, we've taken every effort to ensure we accurately represent our products and services and their ability to improve your life or grow your business. However, there is no guarantee that you will get any results or earn any money using any of our ideas, tools, strategies or recommendations, and we do not purport any "get rich schemes" in any of our content. Nothing in this book is a promise or guarantee of earnings. Your level of success in attaining similar results is dependent upon a number of factors including your skill, knowledge, ability, dedication, business savvy, network, and financial situation, to name a few. Because these factors differ according to individuals, we cannot and do not guarantee your success, income level, or ability to earn revenue. You alone are responsible for your actions and results in life and business. Any forward-looking statements outlined in this book or on our Sites are simply our opinion and thus are not guarantees or promises for actual performance. It should be clear to you that by law we make no guarantees that you will achieve any results from our ideas or models presented in this book or on our Sites, and we offer no professional legal, medical, psychological or financial advice.

CONTENTS

Introduction for Readers of The Kindle Publishing Bible Series

I N THIS BOOK, WE'RE going to cover the key aspects of authorship that all great authors must understand and master in order to become successful. What I want to do is give you the tools you need to succeed. What I don't want to do is just give you a list of to-do's and action steps without giving you the fundamental principles of success that make those action steps work so well. In my other books for authors *The Kindle Publishing Bible* and *The Kindle Writing Bible*, I share best practices and action steps that any author can use to write more books and sell more books.

But in this book I wanted to go beyond strategies and share the principles for success. Why? Because the strategies for success will always change with the times. But the principles of success never change—they are universal. If you rely on the principles of success, you will always be successful—forever! If you rely on someone else's strategies, you will only be successful as long as those strategies work. With so many recent changes at Amazon[1], these principles for success are now more important than ever for authors to understand. Because the publishing world is changing so fast, those who understand these principles will succeed while those who follow old strategies will fail as those strategies become outdated.

Most of the book marketing strategies I share in *The Kindle Publishing Bible* didn't even exist just three years ago! They're all brand new because they came about as a result of the massive changes in eBook publishing and some of the unique features of Search Engine

---

[1] http://www.tckpublishing.com/amazon-kdp-kindle-book-description-html-update/

Optimization and how Amazon bestseller lists and sales rankings work. If you follow the marketing strategies in *The Kindle Publishing Bible* as of 2013, I guarantee you will sell more books. But if you follow those strategies 10 years from now, I can't promise you anything! Who knows if Amazon will even be around in 10 years? I think Amazon will be doing wonderful things 10 years from now—but who knows? It's impossible to predict the future. That's why you shouldn't rely on strategies alone for your success. You must understand and apply these fundamentals of success to become a highly paid author.

Everything I learned about marketing books came to me as a result of my tireless pursuit of success. I learned so much because I did what was necessary to learn it. I stayed up late and I woke up early. I read thousands of books on marketing, publishing, writing, and every area of business, success and psychology you can imagine. I read thousands of blog posts and spent countless hours researching. You can benefit from my labors and make your journey a lot easier by reading books like this—but there is no shortcut to success. You still have to read the book. And when you're done reading it, you still have to apply the new behaviors and strategies. And when those strategies stop working, which they will over the years as things change, you must have your own personal success habits in place that will guarantee your success. You can't rely on me or anyone else to tell you what to do to succeed because strategies change. And if all you have are strategies that used to work without understanding the principles that make them work, you'll be vulnerable when things change. Whatever success you do achieve will be short-lived.

A good example of this is the real estate market. I know several real estate investors who went to seminars and learned all about certain investing strategies. Many of them were millionaires in a very short period of time. Then, when the financial crisis hit in 2007, they all went broke! Why? Because the strategies necessary for success changed, but they didn't change their strategies. They thought they were successful real estate investors, but they were really just copycats. They copied strategies taught to them by their mentors or gurus and they never learned the fundamentals of investing. One of the fundamentals of investing, by the way, is that you should never risk it all. If there's ever a moment where you're at risk of losing everything, you're not investing—you're gambling! I don't want you to gamble with your success. I want to help guarantee your success.

I don't want you to be caught using old and outdated strategies, relying only on other people's systems for your success. That's why I'm teaching you the fundamentals of becoming a successful author. In this book you will learn the principles of success so that you can be successful now and in the future, regardless of what changes come. When the publishing industry changes dramatically again, as it will, you will be ready for the new publishing world. You'll do what it takes to learn how to take advantage of those changes, and you'll be far ahead of the competition.

In this book, you will learn how to develop successful habits that will guarantee you'll take the necessary actions to achieve success in any new environment. While your competitors are busy re-editing a book for the 24th time or complaining about publishers rejecting them, you'll be busy working away at creating your next bestselling book, smiling all the while.

In my other books on publishing and marketing, I gave you the fish—many fish—so that you could eat and be full. I gave you what you wanted—simple, easy-to-use strategies that you can implement right now to sell more books, or write better, or format your books for kindle, and so on. This book is different. I'm going to teach you how to fish so that you will never again wonder how to provide for yourself and your family. I must warn you that in this book, I'm not going to give you what you *want*. In this book, I'm going to give you what you *need*. Trust me, there's a big difference! What most people want is a magic bullet that guarantees overnight success, but what they really need is a strong understanding of the fundamentals that create long-term success.

It's easy to follow someone else's formula for success if it's been well-designed and broken down into simple steps. It's like someone giving you free food—mmm, delicious! We all love free food. But too much free food and you stop working. You get used to it. You get stuck in old habits, and if things change, you might not have anything to eat when all that free fish rots.

It's much harder to learn how to design your own life so that success becomes inevitable. That's what I want for you—success. I want you to be successful no matter what. No excuses! Luckily for you, you're about to learn how to make success inevitable. If you do what it takes, you will be successful and no one nor anything in the world can stop you from achieving the success you dream of. But it's going to take more effort on your part. It's going to take more courage, more strength and more guts than what you're used to.

Maybe that's why I didn't write this book until now. Maybe you weren't ready to learn these advanced strategies for success. Or maybe I wasn't ready to teach them. But either way, here we are now on this journey together. I hope you're ready to study and practice and become a highly paid author!

CHAPTER 1
STARTING WITH WHY

WHY DO YOU WANT TO become a highly paid author? I can show you how to achieve that goal, but unless you understand clearly *why* you want it, you'll give up when the inevitable obstacles and challenges come up.

Without a clear purpose and reason why, you'll be like any other opportunity-seeker who's always looking for a new way to get rich quick but isn't willing to do the work it takes to achieve true, lasting success.

I don't want you to spend your entire life drifting from one "hot new opportunity" to another. I want to help you create lasting success! But you can't do that unless you're absolutely clear about *why you want to become a highly paid author.*

ACTION STEPS

Right now, write down why you want to become a highly paid author in your journal or notebook. Write down every single reason you can think of—the more, the better. Whoever has the biggest list of reasons to become successful wins!

WHY IS MORE IMPORTANT THAN HOW, WHAT, WHEN OR WHERE

Getting clear on why you want to become a highly paid author is more important than the how's, what's, when's and where's. If you're not clear on *why* you're working so hard to become a highly paid author, you'll simply give up when times get tough. When you get knocked down, bruised and bloodied by circumstances outside of your control, you'll be lying on the ground wondering why you would ever want to face such pain *just to become a highly paid author.*

If you have a clear why when you get knocked down, you'll know why it's worth all the pain, effort and work. But if you don't know why, you'll just stay down there in pain. You won't get back up. You won't keep going. You'll quit! Quitting is the #1 cause of failure, and it's the only thing that can stop you from achieving your dreams.

That's why you will never achieve the success you say you want unless you know clearly why you want it. In this book, you're going to learn the how's, what's, where's, and when's of creating a successful business as a highly paid author. And make no mistake about it—becoming a highly paid author is running a business. Your why is the fuel that will keep your business going when other mere mortals would simply give up.

Others have described their why as a purpose, mission, or dharma. It's your driving force in life that gives you reasons to keep going when others would quit. Most people fail in life simply because they quit. They give up. They're just not willing to keep going in the face of failure.

But if you want to become a highly paid author, you will have to be willing to face failure after failure. You'll have to be willing to keep going in spite of what seem like insurmountable odds. That's the only route to success! And trust me, it will be a lot easier once you find your why, your purpose, your mission in life.

ACTION STEPS

Write down in your journal or notebook these questions and then answer them with the first thing that comes to mind. Invest the time in this journaling exercise to discover your true purpose in life and give you the fuel you need to achieve your dreams.

- *If you had a God-given purpose in life, what would it be?*

- *Why is becoming a successful author so important to you?*

- *Are you willing to do whatever it takes to become a highly paid author?*

It might take you some time to come up with the right answers for you. There's no rush! Take your time and realize that you're in control of your life and your destiny.

CHAPTER 2
CREATING SUCCESS HABITS

THROUGHOUT THIS BOOK, WE'LL BE talking mainly about creating the right habits for success and letting go of the old habits that are keeping you stuck, frustrated and unhappy. In this chapter, we're going to briefly discuss habits and how to change them so that you can practice applying these fundamentals of success in your everyday life.

Mastering habit is the absolute key to success in any area of life. Our habits are responsible for over 90% of what we do on a daily basis—and what you do on a daily basis is 100% responsible for the results you achieve in life. Therefore, habits are 100% responsible for what you achieve in life. So mastering your habits should be your #1 priority for success! This entire book is about how to create the right habits for success and eliminate habits that no longer support you in achieving what you want.

Let's start by defining habit in a way that will help you master it. *A habit exists anytime you do something without consciously thinking about it.* In other words, if you do something automatically in any given situation, you have a habit of doing it.

All you need to go from where you are to an entirely new level of success is just 5 or 6 new habits. Just 5 or 6 new habits could completely change your life financially! Chances are, you already have several habits that are leading you in the right direction, but you probably also have a few other habits that are holding you back. When you get rid of those old habits that are holding you back and create 5 or 6 new habits to take you even further, you'll find it effortless and easy to achieve all your financial goals and dreams. The challenge is to correctly determine which habits to change and which new habits to adopt, and to do the work required to make those new habits stick. That's what you'll be learning in this book.

As you continue to read, you'll be presented with many opportunities to eliminate old habits and adopt new ones. I would urge you to focus on one or two key habits at a time. Don't try to change *everything* all at once. It's much easier to focus your efforts on one major change, and once that new change has become a habit, move on to your next habit change. If you keep repeating this process, you'll find yourself achieving higher levels of success and fulfillment every year, and you'll be able to achieve far more than you ever imagined.

You must understand that habits are created over long periods of time. The habits you have today took weeks, months or even years to develop—both the good habits that lead you toward success and the bad ones that hold you back. So don't think that you will be able to change every habit overnight. You won't! But you can *start today*. You can start making changes today, and you will see results quickly if you continue making changes. You can't use your habits as an excuse not achieving your dreams if you're not willing to start changing your habits *right now.*

Realize that habits are situation-based. This means that in different situations, different habits may exist. For example, you may drive to work and find that when you arrive you have forgotten the entire trip and aren't really sure how you got there. Driving to work has become a habit—you did it unconsciously! But if I were to take you to another city in another country where they drive on the other side of the road and you have no idea where you are, you would NOT be navigating unconsciously. You wouldn't have to relearn how to drive the car, but you would definitely have to relearn how to drive on the other side of the road and how to navigate in a new environment.

This simple analogy should help you understand how important the environment is on your habits. Put yourself in a different environment, and your old habits will either disappear, change or stay the same depending on the situation. This does NOT mean that the habits no longer exist; they just may not apply to that new situation.

Here you can see one of the most important principles for changing habits or creating new habits:

> *To change a habit or create a new habit,*
> *change the environment.*

Now, this principle seems easy to understand and obvious, but it's a bit trickier than it may first appear. Here's why: there really is no such thing as the "environment". You see, the "environment" in which you see yourself is determined by two parts: 1) the actual physical environment around you and 2) how you perceive the environment.

For example, let's say that you have a habit of answering your phone every time it rings, regardless of who you're with or what you're doing at the time. Let's assume that this habit occurs 100% of the time, in every situation, no matter what. It's a real habit.

Next, let's pretend that you're in a crowded, fancy restaurant, enjoying a wonderful meal with some close friends. You're all having a wonderful time chatting and laughing when all of a sudden your phone rings. But you don't hear it ring because you're so engrossed in the conversation. Because you didn't hear it ring, you didn't pick it up. The habit didn't work! Even though the physical environment, or stimulus as scientists refer to it, was the correct environment for that habit to express itself, you didn't pick up the phone. And the reason you didn't express the habit is because *you did not perceive the stimulus.* Had you perceived that your phone was ringing, you would have certainly picked it up. But since you didn't perceive it, you went on chatting happily with your friends instead.

Thus, you can see that the environment itself is not as important as your perception of the environment. Your perception is what will determine when your habits are activated and when they are not.

So now you have two tools for changing habits:

1) Change the environment.
2) Change your perception.

Let's explore now how you can use each of these strategies to creating lasting habit changes.

Changing Your Environment

Whether you like it or not, much of what you do on a daily basis is determined by your environment. Very rarely do you actually exercise "free will" to do something new. Most of the time, you just follow old habits based on the information you perceive in your environment.

Luckily, it's pretty easy to make changes in your environment. But before we discuss making changes in your environment, we must discuss another principle of habits:

> *Habits are easier to create*
> *than they are to change or eliminate.*

Because of the way neurons in our brains connect and function, it's far easier to create new neuron connections in the brain than it is to erase or remove old ones. That's why it's much easier to create a new habit than it is to get rid of an old habit. In fact, the only way to truly get rid of an old habit is to "imprint" a new habit on top of the old habit, thereby changing the connections of neurons in your brain.

Let's pretend you drink coffee every morning and it's a strong habit that you would like to change. Instead of trying to eliminate the habit, it would be much easier to simply create a new habit instead. So instead of drinking coffee every morning when you wake up, you could drink tea or water instead. Because the change is so small, and because you're keeping the environment largely the same, it's much easier to develop the "drink water every morning habit" than it is to remove the "drink coffee every morning habit". And, if you drink water each morning instead of coffee, eventually that old coffee habit will be gone—those neurons in your brain will be programmed for drinking water every morning instead of coffee. And when that happens, your new behavior will be just as automatic as drinking coffee every morning is for you now. You won't even have to think about it!

You see, that is the beauty of habit. Once a habit is there, you no longer have to think about it. If you have developed a good habit of writing every single day, you no longer have to think about it. It's automatic. You've become programmed to write every day. Understanding this, I hope you can now see why becoming a highly paid author is just as easy as being a broke writer. *The only difference is your daily routine which is determined by your habits.* Once the right habits are in place, creating success becomes very easy and automatic.

And once a habit exists, it's difficult to change. So once you've created a new success habit, it becomes very hard to NOT become successful. You've become programmed for success, in other words. The point of this book is to help you program yourself for success. And once you do that, success will become just as easy and automatic as driving to work has been for you. It won't even be difficult! But it will be difficult in the beginning to change your habits—that's where you must focus your energy and effort.

How To Change Your Environment

Now it's time to learn how to change your environment.

There are many ways you can change your environment to help with habit formation and habit change, but the key is to focus on simplicity. Try to find the simplest, easiest way to change the environment. For example, if you have a habit of being distracted at home when you try to write, it might be easiest to just write outside of your home.

Maybe you can go to a local café or library to get some peace and quiet and avoid interruptions. It may not be the *best* solution, but it's the *easiest* solution oftentimes. Maybe the "best solution" is to buy a new home with a private office that has soundproof walls, doors and windows, and put a sign on the door that lets you family know they are never to interrupt you while you write. But the best solution may not be easily accomplished right now. Instead, just go for the easiest solution.

> *When it comes to changing habits, go for the easiest solution; keep it simple and avoid complicated or costly changes if possible!*

The easier the solution is, the easier and more quickly you will develop your new habit, and the easier and more quickly you will achieve the success you're looking for.

Other common ways writers have changed their environment to help them become more successful include:

❖ *Setting an alarm clock to wake up earlier each day to write in the morning.*

❖ *Staying up later to write in the late evening when everyone else is asleep.*

❖ *Writing everything that comes to mind first in one session, and not editing until the writing session is complete. This helps you write faster and avoid over-editing or getting stuck in a cycle of ineffectiveness.*

❖ *Creating an "editing limit" so that you don't get stuck in a habit of constantly editing old material without producing new material.*

CHANGING YOUR PERCEPTION

Changing your perception is the method of habit change that is least often employed, which is a shame since it's the most powerful method for habit change of all. The reason most people never think of changing their perception to change their habits is because they don't have the tools or strategies to do so. You will no longer have the luxury of using that excuse after reading this section.

There are many ways you can change your perception, but the most powerful way is to change your beliefs, perspective and attitude.

> *Your beliefs are how you THINK*
> *about the world.*
>
> *Your perspective is how you SEE the world.*
>
> *Your attitude is how you FEEL about the world*

When you change how you think, how you see, and how you feel about a given situation, it becomes much easier to change what you *do* in that given situation. That's how changing your beliefs, perspective and attitude can make habit change much easier.

Your beliefs, perspective and attitude are often intertwined, and you will find that changing one will often change the others. For example, if you have a bad attitude about how most publishers earn more royalties than authors do because you believe the creator of a book should be paid more than the publisher, your belief might change if you could see how much work the publisher does. A simple change in your perspective could immediately change your beliefs and attitude about publishers.

Undoubtedly, you've had several moments in your life where a new perspective changed your beliefs or attitude about certain people or certain situations. The problem is, most of the time this just happens by accident. *The key to creating success is to intentionally change your beliefs, attitudes, and perspective.* Here's how:

I know how much work a publisher does because I've done it! Except not lately with Amazon/Kindle.

> *Ask yourself questions that will give you new perspectives,*
> *beliefs, and attitudes.*

I'll admit, when someone first told me to ask myself questions, I thought it was ridiculous. Why would I ask myself a question if I already know what I know? But the truth is, most of what we know is unconscious.

Asking questions makes that inner knowledge become conscious so that we can use it to improve our lives. You have more knowledge, wisdom, courage, and intelligence inside you than you can possibly imagine—the key is unlocking it. And asking questions is a simple and effective way to do just that.

Questions are by far the most powerful form of learning and creating change in your life. That's why the Socratic Method was used so successfully thousands of years ago. Socrates wasn't a fool—he understood the power of asking the right questions. Today, however, we study boring textbooks and few teachers use the Socratic Method anymore. Who knows why?

Here is a list of some of the most powerful questions I've ever heard for creating immediate and lasting changes in your beliefs, attitudes, perspective and habits.

ACTION STEPS

Take out your notebook or journal and write down these questions. Answer them each time you have a habit to change or a problem to overcome.

What can I do today to increase my income?

Looking back on my day, if I lived every remaining day of my life just like that, would I achieve the success I wish to achieve in the next 1 year, 5 years, 10 years? If not, why not? What would I change about this day to ensure I achieved the success I desire over the next several years?

Is what I'm doing working? Is it leading me down the right path?

Will this activity or behavior inevitably lead to my success and achievement of my intended goals?

Am I doing the right thing right now? Is there something more important I could be doing to help me achieve my goals?

What don't I see? Is there anything that could happen that could entirely ruin my plans or intended purpose? If so, what could I do to prevent those bad things from happening?

Will I regret making this decision in 1 year, 5 years, 10 years?

Will I regret not making this decision in 1 year, 5 years, 10 years?

Does this have to be perfect or is it good enough? If it's not quite good enough, could I keep making forward progress anyway and fix any mistakes that come up later?

Am I sabotaging my own success? If so, how? Could I stop doing that?

Will this even matter in 10 years?

Am I having fun and doing what I love? If not, why not? Could I put more fun and love into what I'm doing right now?

Should I take advice from this person? Have they been successful in the area they are giving me advice about?

Just because it seems like everyone else is doing things this way, does that mean I have to do it the same way? Is there a better way to do it for me?

Do I really care what people think or say about me or am I more concerned with what I want for my own life?

Is this the most valuable use of my time? Are there higher priority activities I could be doing instead?

Is this a big deal or a small issue? If it's a small issue, should I just do it to get it done with or would another course of action be better?

Is this problem/challenge worth getting upset about? Will I even remember it a year from now?

Do I really need to do (insert activity/routine that you do regularly)?

Is it time to walk away and try something new?

Why am I doing what I am doing with my life?

When will I start taking my own advice?

If money were not an issue, what would I do with my life?

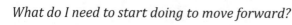

What do I need to start doing to move forward?

What do I need to stop doing to move forward?

Am I doing everything possible to achieve my goals and if not, why not?

Am I living my life in a way that makes me happy and makes the people around me that I love happy?

What would I do if today were my last day?

What would I do if I was not afraid?

Can I do better?

What have I done to make a difference?

Invest the time in asking and answering these questions. The greatest resource in the world for improving your life is you! I recommend using that resource more often and more wisely by asking yourself the right questions.

For more information about habits and how to change them, I highly recommend reading *The Power of Habit*[2] by Charles Duhigg.

---

[2] http://www.amazon.com/Power-Habit-What-Life-Business/dp/1400069289

CHAPTER 3
DOING WHAT'S EASY AND WHAT'S DIFFICULT

WRITING IS INCREDIBLY EASY. IF you're reading this book now on a Kindle, chances are you have the ability to write at anytime, anywhere, night and day. Within a few feet of you right now, you probably have access to pens, pencils, paper, a computer with a Word processor, and a smartphone or tablet device that you could write on as well while you are on the go. If that doesn't make writing easy enough for you, there's now dictation software such as Dragon Naturally Speaking and others which can turn your spoken words into writing—instantly!

On top of that, there are dozens of free voice recording apps for Androids, iPhones and any other tablet or smartphone that will record you speaking which you can then have transcribed cheaply and easily on any one of a few thousand websites.

In the business world, we talk about "barriers to entry." Barriers to entry are basically the costs or challenges involved in entering a business, market or niche. The barriers to entry of becoming a writer are virtually nonexistent for those of you reading this book. Sure, there are some people on Planet Earth who still don't have access to a computer or the internet, and a very small few who have no access to pen and paper. And, of course, there are millions of people who are still illiterate. But I'm guessing you don't have any of those problems—so there are no "barriers to entry" for you to becoming a writer.

There are, however, significant challenges you will face along the way. Much of this book is devoted to helping you overcome those challenges, which we will cover in much more detail later on, including:

- ❖ Fear
- ❖ Procrastination
- ❖ Financial Challenges (how to earn a living as a writer)
- ❖ "Writer's Block"
- ❖ Ignorance (not knowing what to do or how to do it)
- ❖ Competition (there are millions of writers and very few actually earn more than minimum wage, while most earn far less)
- ❖ Distractions and Interruptions
- ❖ Being Alone (not having a team)
- ❖ Being Unknown
- ❖ Not Having Connections to Publishers, Agents or Industry Influencers
- ❖ Not Being "Good Enough" At Writing

These are just a few of the obstacles and challenges you will face along your journey to becoming a highly paid writer. The truth is that we all face challenges and obstacles when we begin any endeavor, and writing is no exception to this simple rule of life.

When I started writing my first book I was 19 years old, studying business in college. I had no connections to publishers or agents, no formal training as a writer, and no idea what I was doing. All I knew is that I enjoyed writing and had a message to share with the world—so I was going to write my book or die trying!

Luckily, I survived despite my complete lack of knowledge of writing and publishing. And now I am a bestselling author because of those earlier writing efforts—because I chose to write even though I had no idea what I was doing or how I would ever get the book published, let alone get paid.

You see, there will always be challenges and struggles when you attempt anything great in life. The key then is not to shy away from obstacles or challenges, but to learn to overcome them. We all start out knowing nothing. We all start from "zero —that place of complete ignorance. In order to succeed as a writer, you have to have the guts to begin writing without trying to look good. You don't have to be the best writer in the world. At TCK Publishing, we hire the best editors in the world to fix the mistakes made by our clients, some of whom understand very little about writing professionally. Why do we do this? Because we know that writing a bestselling book and getting a book finished has very little to do with writing skill on the author's part—it has everything to do with having the guts to write a great book in the first place.

Now, I'm not saying that anyone can push a few buttons in Microsoft Word, get published and become a bestselling author without any original ideas, thoughts or talent. What I am saying is that *all the talent in the world is utterly useless if you don't have the guts to write and publish a book in the first place.*

If I had to put this idea into a mathematical equation, it would look like this:

> ### Willingness to Write a Book > Writing Talent

Having the willingness to write a book is far more important than having superb writing talent. The truth is, without being willing to start writing, you'll never become a truly great writer!

Malcolm Gladwell in his bestselling book *Outliers* shares how it takes about 10,000 hours of practice for people to become masters at a skill. Whether it be playing violin like Vivaldi, becoming a business tycoon like Bill Gates, or becoming a hockey superstar like Wayne Gretsky, it takes a lot of time invested in practice to become truly great at something. Gladwell goes into great detail in the book to show that it's not natural talent that creates the world's best athletes, businessmen, and artists. Instead the world's best are created through practice.

Therefore, with enough time, energy, and devotion, any of us can become great at anything we choose. So if you want to become a great writer, one of the world's best, all you have to do is spend 10,000 hours *practicing* writing.

Fortunately, or unfortunately, the only way to practice writing is to actually write. And the best way to become a better writer is to write what you actually want to write about. That means, for most of us, writing a book. You can write a lot of books in 10,000 hours and get paid handsomely on your way to becoming a master.

Even if you're a brand new writer, don't sell yourself short. Start writing your own books, even if you have to do freelance work just to make ends meet. You will be much more inspired to get up every day and write if you are writing your own book which you have chosen to write than if you are hired as a ghostwriter or to write some research reports for a third party.

Take two writers. Let them each write for 10,000 hours. One of them is a ghostwriter or freelance writer. She writes what other people tell her to write, and she does a great job at it. The other writer writes her own books. She writes what she wants, when she wants, as she wants. She has pretty much complete control over what she writes, subject to feedback from editors, publishers, and readers, if any.

I guarantee you that the second writer will be much more successful, happier and paid more than the first. Why? *Because writing is primarily an art and secondarily a mechanical task.* And great art comes from great inspiration.

There are two parts to writing—the art of writing and the mechanics of writing. Personally, I have very little skill when it comes to the mechanics of writing. I don't know the difference between APA and MLA, and I have no idea what those letters even stand for. Like I said before, my publishing company hires great writers to understand and fix the mechanical side of writing. It's very easy to find great mechanical writers who understand every rule and nuiance of English (or just about any other language for those of you who wish to write in other languages). What is much harder to find is writers who are great at the art of writing, writers who burn with a passion to birth great books.

When I say writing is an art, you must understand that art is entirely subjective. Let's say you and I tour an art museum together. We both look at a painting on the wall. You see a magnificent work of art—a breathtaking piece that leaves you in awe. I see some paint smeared on a canvas and can't possibly see how that could be called art. Thus is the subjectivity of art.

The same holds true for writing. This is why so many authors get rejected by hundreds of publishers until, finally, one day they get their lucky break and someone agrees to publish them. Then they go on to sell millions of copies. Is it because that manuscript which was rejected by hundreds of publishers magically got better? No! It's because a publisher saw something in that manuscript that others could not see.

You see, art is subjective. And, at the end of the day, the only people who can really determine whether art is any good are those who spend their time looking at art. In the publishing industry, we call those people readers. And they are the only people who will determine how much your art is worth. Publishers, agents and editors are just experts who have an opinion, but at the end of the day it's the opinion of readers that really matters.

Because writing is an art that takes 10,000 hours of practice to master, you're going to be producing a lot of really bad art. Van Gogh painted thousands of canvasses in his lifetime. He died poor, the public completely unaware of his talent until after he died. He was so poor that he would give away paintings in return for a meal at times. Those same paintings later sold for millions of dollars. But even Van Gogh painted bad pictures, especially in his earlier days. Even the masters made mistakes. In fact, that's how they became masters—by making lots and lots of mistakes.

The funny thing is, no one remembers Van Gogh's artistic mistakes, although everyone seems to remember him cutting his own ear off. But no one sits around in the art world and talks about how bad Van Gogh's second painting was. No one laughs at his horrible early mistakes. They only remember his successes—his masterpieces. The same will hold true for you, my writer friend.

If you want to become a highly paid writer and a great writer, you must be willing to write a lot of really bad stuff. You must be willing to write garbage, a horrible compilation of words which would embarrass your mother and cause your father to wonder why you don't just get a real job! Because if you're not willing to write poorly at first, you will never, ever, *ever* become a great writer.

If you want to be great at anything, you must be willing to be really bad at it *at first.* Don't stay bad forever! But that's where you must begin. Then you must start practicing. And studying. And practicing what you've studied. And studying what you've practiced. For 10,000 hours or so. Then you will become a truly great writer.

The difference between writing and other art forms, though, is that you can hire an editor to help fix your mistakes. This is why many authors can have their first novel or first nonfiction book published easily. That's very different than a painter! Can you imagine having your first painting on display at the Louvre, or even just a local art gallery? I remember my first painting—it was hideous!

Unfortunately, you can't hire a painting editor to erase and correct some of your poor brush strokes. You can, however, hire an editor to fix your writing mistakes. This is the key difference between writing and all other art forms, and it's the reason so many "unskilled" writers sell millions of books, while some of the greatest skilled writers of our time spend all their time editing books and have no published works of their own.

In fact, if you look at the bestselling authors in the world right now and the editors who edited those books, you'll find 90% of the time that the editor has more training, experience and knowledge of the writing profession than the author!

This brings us to the Golden Rule of Authorship:

> *It doesn't matter how good your first draft is—what matters is the finished product.*

I call this the Golden Rule of Authorship because it is true now, forever, and always, and the understanding of this simple truth will lead you on the golden path to riches if you use it wisely.

You see, readers buy the finished product, not the first draft! And no one cares whether the author understands MLA or APA or how well-written the first draft was; readers only care about the book they buy, the finished product. They see nothing and know nothing of the process that went into creating the final product. That's why it really doesn't matter how you get to the finished product (as long as you do it legally and ethically)—you can do it by yourself or hire an editor, or a team of editors to get you there. All that matters is the finished product, the final version of the book.

Now, because writing is an art first and a mechanical skill second, and because you can hire very skilled writers to polish your final product to perfection, and because this can all be done incredibly cheaply today, the barriers to entry of creating a book are incredibly small—so small that my 4 year old niece could become a published author in about a week. And because these barriers are so small, the competition is enormous. And because the competition is enormous, most authors who have created wonderful books never sell more than 100 copies. And because most books never sell more than 100 copies, most authors are very poor. And so, my friend, if you want to become a highly paid author, you must come to the inevitable conclusion that writing a book alone is not going to get you there.

Writing a good book is "necessary but not sufficient" as my mother once said. You must write a good book to become a highly paid author (better yet, you must write several great books). But having a good book alone will not get you paid highly, or even at all.

There are a few more steps to getting those huge royalty checks flowing into your bank account.

In order to become a highly paid writer, you must follow the formula:

> #1. Write a good book.
>
> #2. Publish the book.
>
> #3. Market the book.

Authors who focus only on #1 stay broke.

Authors who focus on #1 and #2 will get paid modestly, or very well if they are lucky like J. K. Rowling.

Authors who focus on #1, #2 and #3 will be paid highly, even without luck.

This is why I say that writing is easy and also really, really difficult. It's very easy to do #1. Just about anyone with a little knowledge, time and effort can write a book and hire a great editor. Getting your book published and marketing your book can be much more difficult, for a variety of reasons:

❖ *The skills it takes to write a book are very different from the skills it takes to publish and market a book.*

❖ *The barriers to entry of writing a book are almost nonexistent, but the barriers to publishing and marketing a book are astronomical in comparison.*

❖ *Most writers get exhausted just writing the book and aren't willing to learn how to publish and market it.*

The good news is that these obstacles exist to help you in many ways! First of all, these obstacles keep many other would-be highly paid authors from competing. The truth is, most people just give up before they ever reach their goals. The path is too difficult, or they're just not that interested, and so they quit. That's why so many authors are willing to write books or become ghostwriters while so few are willing to learn how to publish and market their books.

But the other blessing you get from the struggle is the journey. Your journey from humble writer to bestselling author will be a fantastic journey, full of wonderful memories and challenges to overcome. Let's be honest—if becoming a highly paid author was so easy that anyone could do it in a week, it wouldn't be worth it. If all you had to do was write a decent book, and then you got paid millions of dollars without doing any more work, it wouldn't be worth it. It would be like running a marathon, and then being announced the winner after 10 seconds. Yeah, it sounds nice to be the winner of the race... but honestly, did you even enjoy the race? Do you feel proud of being the winner? Of course not! It's a hollow achievement. There's no meaning behind it, precisely because you didn't have to struggle to get there. It was just too easy. Becoming a highly paid author is like running a marathon; it's going to take some time and a whole lot of effort, but when you get there it will all be worth it.

That's why you're lucky to be on the path you're on to becoming a highly paid author. Because it's NOT too easy. It's not too difficult either. It's the perfect mix. If you're willing to do what it takes to succeed, you will never regret your decision to take this path.

CHAPTER 4
HOW TO OVERCOME THE SUCCESS OBSTACLE COURSE

OBSTACLES COME UP FOR ALL of us on a daily basis. Instead of seeing obstacles as "bad" or "wrong" or "unfair", you ought to look at them as blessings. Obstacles are blessings because they give you the opportunity to learn, grow, overcome and make progress.

No great success was ever achieved without overcoming a lot of obstacles along the way. In society today, many of us are programmed from an early age that obstacles and mistakes should be avoided. In school, if you raise your hand and get the wrong answer, other kids laugh at you. If you get the wrong answer on a test, you get a bad grade and might even be held back a year. But in real life everyone makes mistakes and everyone is faced with a never-ending stream of obstacles.

Instead of avoiding obstacles in fear, you ought to embrace the challenge with courage. Realize that all authors face many, many obstacles before they ever become bestsellers. The ones who don't get past the obstacles just stay where they are. If you want to make progress, then simply move past the next obstacle, and the next, and so on.

Many obstacles in life you will just have to learn to overcome by yourself or with the help of your team. But there are many obstacles that seem to be universal for most writers. So right now we're going to cover the most common obstacles authors face and show you how to overcome them as quickly as possible so that you can start selling more books as quickly as possible.

WHAT TO DO WHEN YOU DON'T FEEL LIKE WRITING

If you're anything like me, you will find yourself from time to time having the opportunity to write and maybe even thinking that you *should* be writing but *you won't feel like it.* At these times, your mind will probably be coming up with a million excuses as to why you shouldn't be writing such as:

> "I don't feel like it."
>
> "I'm not in the right mood to write."
>
> "I don't need to write right now."
>
> "I don't have anything to write."
>
> "I just want to rest."
>
> "I should take a break."

What do you do when you know you should do something, but you don't feel like doing it? This doesn't just apply to writing—it could apply to marketing, editing, attending social events, relationships or any other area of life.

Here's how to get back on track when you don't feel like doing what it takes to succeed:

JUST GIVE IT A TRY

Just give it a try! This is one of the best ways to overcome this obstacle to your success. You say to yourself, "Even though I don't feel like writing right now, I'm going to give it a try for just 5 minutes and see how it feels." It's a lot easier to do something for just a few minutes than for a few hours. And oftentimes, all that's happening is that we're associating more pain with writing than with not writing.

So if you can decrease the potential pain by decreasing the commitment, it makes it a lot easier to get started. And once you get started, you tend to continue. It's cliché, but 80% of success is just showing up. That means getting started!

You could use the same strategy for other times when you don't feel like doing something that you know you should do. If you've had a fight with your spouse and know you should apologize but don't feel like fighting anymore, then just say to yourself, "I'm just going to try for 5 minutes to apologize, and if it doesn't work, it's okay—I'll just walk away after 5 minutes and we can talk more later." It's a lot easier to walk into a 5-minute conversation than an hour-long fight with your spouse.

This same strategy works exceptionally well for other issues too. Let's say there's a big networking event in town and you think it would be a good idea to go for business purposes, but you're not really feeling like socializing. Then just tell yourself, "Even though I don't feel like going to the networking event, I'm going to attend for just 30 minutes and say hello to a few people. Then, if I want to go back home, I can."

The reason this strategy works so well is because it lowers your resistance to the activity or behavior you know is good for you but might not feel like doing. Although we humans love to pretend that we think logically, the truth is we make decisions with emotion and then justify them later with logic. And oftentimes these emotional decisions aren't even based on facts or logic at all!

For example, you might think that apologizing to your spouse would just start another fight that would drag on for hours or days, but you have no way of knowing that ahead of time. It could just be a simple 5-minute conversation where both of you are left feeling much happier and relieved of all that tension that had built up. But in our mind, that simple 5-minute conversation turns into an ordeal that lasts for hours.

We see ourselves fighting, we think of what to say to get back at the person and we think of all the reasons we'll use to justify our position.

And all that "thinking" we're doing is just making it harder to solve the problem and move on with our lives!

One of the best ways to get something done that you don't feel like doing is to lower your resistance to it by lowering your initial commitment. Just give it a try!

CHANGE YOUR STATE

What do you do if things don't go well after you've given it a try? Maybe you sat down for 5 minutes and started writing but you don't feel like it anymore. What do you do then? Just give up? No!

There are several things you can do. First of all, you might want to take a short walk, do some exercise, breathe some fresh air, or do something to change your physical state. Our bodies influence our thoughts and behavior, and oftentimes we get into a bad "posture" physically. This could be slouching, frowning, looking down, or some unidentified physical behavior that you only notice by not feeling well, being bored, or feeling uneasy. Usually, all we need to get back into a positive, resourceful and productive state is just to move our bodies and relieve that tension.

Try walking or running around the house or neighborhood a few times to change your state. Start doing some jumping jacks or pushups until you get your heart rate up. Put on your favorite music as loud as you like and dance around for a few minutes. Just move your body!

You'll be amazed how just a little moving and grooving can completely change how you feel and help you get back on track to being productive in just a few minutes.

NEGATIVE PEOPLE AND DREAM KILLERS

Dealing with negative people and dream killers is another huge stumbling block for many would-be successful authors. If you let someone kill your dream of becoming a successful author, then you probably don't care enough to begin with. You must listen to your own inner voice and ignore the voices of others who would try to stop you from living your life's true purpose. Let your inner voice guide you and don't be swayed by the voices of outside opinion.

For many, it's the people closest to us who can be the biggest negative influence. Maybe you have parents, siblings or other close relatives who ridicule you or try to convince you to give up your dream and "get a real job." If you really want to be a successful author, stop listening to these people. Ignore them. Avoid them if at all possible.

You can't live a great life surrounding yourself with people who constantly put you down and try to kill your dreams. You must choose either your dream or your dream killers.

NEGATIVE OR HARSH REVIEWS

The day the first caveman created the first rock painting, the critic was born. The caveman critic said, "That's the ugliest thing I've ever seen! Who do you think you are drawing pictures on the wall?" Art has grown and blossomed in incredible ways since then, but most critics have not.

When you get a negative review or someone tells you your work sucks, just let it go. I know, it hurts. It feels horrible. It's like having someone take a wrench to your stomach and twist it until you just want to lay in bed and cry all day long. But you've got to pick yourself back up and get back to work. Critics say bad things about the work artists do because they're too afraid to create something new themselves. They're looking for acceptance and they try to feel important by denying acceptance of your work.

If you're really paying attention and you can think clearly through your emotional reaction to a negative review, you just might learn something. We all have areas for growth and improvement, and many times a negative review can provide that crucial feedback to help us grow and improve as authors.

So don't shy away from negative feedback. Instead, embrace it and learn from it. And when you're done learning from it, let it go and move on. You've got more books in you—don't stop just because someone who's not willing to write a book says you're not good enough. Obviously you're good enough because you already wrote a book!

FEAR

Franklin Roosevelt said:

> *"There's nothing to fear except fear itself."*

What if that's true?

Most people use fear the wrong way. They use fear as a sign to turn away, stop, or give up. When you're afraid of what others might think if you finished a book, you'll find all kinds of excuses and reasons not to finish it. What if, instead of using fear as a reason to give up, you used it as a reason to keep going? Most of the time, fear is a sign that you're on the right path.

We're only afraid when we're doing something new or something different, or if we believe that we might fail. But doing something different and new where you might fail is the ONLY way to make progress in life. Therefore, fear is actually a wonderful sign—it's a sign that you're growing and making progress. So next time you're feeling afraid to write something new or promote your books, just think "Aha! That fear is a wonderful sign that I'm moving in the right direction."

You can't get rid of fear. It will always come up when we're doing something new or different or risky. Despite the new age philosophy that "fear is just an illusion", it sure doesn't feel like an illusion.

Instead of trying to get rid of fear or run away from it, just accept it for what it is. It's just a sign that you're doing something new.

> *People who let fear rule their lives*
> *never accomplish anything great.*

If you want to accomplish something great with your life, then get used to fear. Let it become your old friend and guide on your journey to success.

PROCRASTINATION

Procrastination is a vice that will rob you blind and leave your family poor and starving if you don't conquer it. There is no virtue in procrastination. It's a habit of thinking and behaving that keeps you stuck.

When writers say they have writer's block, 99% of the time they really just have a bad habit of procrastination. "Writer's block" doesn't exist in reality. It's a euphemism for a mental state of procrastination and lazy thinking.

Many writers use a lack of *inspiration* as an excuse not to write. Well, if that's been a problem for you, I hope these quotes from great writers will cure you of your procrastination:

> *"I can't explain inspiration. A writer is either compelled to write or not. And if I waited for inspiration I wouldn't really be a writer."*
> **Toni Morrison**

"I have learned, as has many another better writer, to summon inspiration to my call as soon as I begin my day's stint, and not to hang around waiting for it. Inspiration is merely a pretty phrase for the zest to work. And it can be cultivated by anyone who has the patience to try. Inspiration that will not come at its possessor's summons is like a dog that cannot be trained to obey. The sooner both are gotten rid of, the better."

Albert Payson Terhune

"All this about inspiration... I think writing is mainly work. Like a mechanic's job. A mechanic might as well say he was waiting for inspiration before he greased your car because if he didn't feel just right he'd miss a lot of the grease points, that he had to feel right up to it."

E.B. White

"There are those . . . who think that the man who works with his imagination should allow himself to wait till—inspiration moves him. When I have heard such doctrine preached, I have hardly been able to repress my scorn. To me it would not be more absurd if the shoemaker were to wait for inspiration, or the tallow-chandler for the divine moment of melting."

Anthony Trollope

> *"Had I mentioned to someone around 1795 that I planned to write, anyone with any sense would have told me to write for two hours every day, with or without inspiration. Their advice would have enabled me to benefit from the ten years of my life I totally wasted waiting for inspiration."*
>
> **Stendhal [Marie-Henri Beyle]**

> *"I don't wait for inspiration. I'm not, in fact, quite sure what inspiration is, but I'm sure that if it is going to turn up, my having started work is the precondition of its arrival."*
>
> **Quentin Blake**

Procrastination can be quickly overcome by developing the habits of proactivity and conscious thinking. When you're proactive, you make decisions and take actions quickly.

When you have a great idea for your next novel or book idea, you write it down **immediately**. When someone mentions a good book about how to be a better writer, you go buy it immediately. When any opportunity comes by for you to improve yourself and your work, you seize that opportunity right away! That's being proactive.

Others may condemn such actions as greedy or excessively ambitious, but those are just labels used by those who don't understand your true purpose in life.

Procrastination is practically encouraged in our society today. Your friends and family will tell you, "It's okay, you had a long day. You don't need to write, just relax." Of course, they only mean well for you. They want you to be happy. But, the truth is you won't feel truly happy and fulfilled "relaxing", watching TV and making small talk instead of living your dreams.

> *There is no happiness in this world that can compete*
> *with living an inspired life.*

If you feel inspired to write, if you hear that little voice inside you say it's time to get to work, don't let anyone talk you out of it. Sit down and write! That little voice inside you is your soul calling you. Listen to its call. It won't steer you wrong.

FINANCIAL CHALLENGES

Most writers struggle their whole lives to earn a decent living as a writer. Many writers have to pinch pennies and work all hours of the day just to get by. But don't ever blame writing for your lack of financial success!

It's almost depressing talking about finances with most artists and writers these days. It seems like almost every author and writer I meet has been indoctrinated with the "starving artist" myth. What a bunch of ~~bullshit~~ lies!

Artists aren't meant to be poor, and many artists do incredibly well financially. Just look at any celebrity. All celebrities are artists. In fact, the richest people in the world are artists—actors and actresses, bestselling authors, and even entrepreneurs. If you don't think being an entrepreneur is an art, then I'd like to see you start a company that employs thousands of people! Trust me, it took Steve Jobs just as much skill and talent to build Apple as it did Michelangelo to paint the Sistine Chapel or J.K. Rowling to write Harry Potter.

As a committed and dedicated author, your peers include some of the wealthiest, most financially successful people on the planet! Here is just a small list of incredibly successful authors who have achieved incredible wealth from writing from $12 Million to over $1 billion:

JK Rowling, Candy Spelling, Stephen King, Danielle Steel, Tom Clancy, Olivia Harrison, James Patterson, John Grisham, Jackie Collins, Michael Crichton, Nora Roberts, Stephenie Meyer, Dean Koontz, Mary Higgins Clark, Dan Brown, Janet Evanovich, Clive Cussler, Jonathan Franzen, Gary Larson, Anne Rice, Carole Radziwill, Stieg Larsson, Ken Follett, Terry McMillan, Jonathan Kellerman, Jon Krakauer, Nicholas Sparks, George R.R. Martin, Harlan Coben, Jack Canfield, Million, Nelson DeMille, Cecily von Ziegesar, Elizabeth Gilbert, Leigh Anne Tuohy, Toni Morrison, Nick Hornby, Pattie Mallette, Leeza Gibbons, David Chilton, Brad Meltzer, Martin Handford, Joe Eszterhas, Nancy Grace, Dr. Cindy Trimm, Tim Ferriss, E.L. James, Million, Patricia Cornwell, Salman Rushdie, Terry Goodkind, Suzanne Collins, and Paulo Coelho.

So you see, there are many artists and writers who are very successful financially. Instead of seeing yourself destined for a life of poverty as an artist, you ought to see yourself destined for a life of wealth and financial abundance, because you are if you dedicate your life to become a great author. If at any point in time you find yourself "starving" as an artist, it's because you chose to live that way. Any day you choose, you can make a new decision and create financial abundance.

IGNORANCE

Ignorance is simply a state of not knowing, a lack of knowledge. We were all born ignorant, and we slowly grow and learn throughout our lives. So if you haven't yet learned how to write a book, or how to get published, or how to market and sell your books effectively, that's okay. You're human. Every great author was once in your shoes.

Every single bestselling author in the world started out ignorant. But then they decided to start learning and start writing. Success didn't come overnight for other authors and it won't come instantly for you either. But it will come if you start learning and start writing and always strive to make progress.

> *If you don't know how to write a book,*
> *you can learn.*
> *If you don't know how to publish a book,*
> *you can learn.*
> *If you don't know how to market a book,*
> *you can learn.*

You can learn anything you want! But in order to learn, you must study. If you want to learn how to write a book, study writing. If you want to learn how to publish a book, study publishing. If you want to learn how to market a book, study marketing. Do you know how many authors actually make studying these three areas a habit? Very few! That's why so few succeed.

COMPETITION

Here's a fact: there are millions of writers and very few actually earn more than minimum wage, while most earn far less than minimum wage.

Here's another fact: half of all writers earn less than the average writer earns.

Neither of these facts actually matter! Why? Because these facts were long true before other authors became bestsellers and started earning massive royalty checks. If they can do it, you can do it. Looking at financial statistics may be depressing, but only because most people aren't willing to do what it takes to become truly great at something. If you're willing to do what it takes to become great at what you do, you'll rise to the top in any field.

The truth is, there's almost no competition at the highest levels of writing. When Twilight became popular, did readers say, "Oh, I don't need to buy Harry Potter anymore, we have Twilight now!" No one has ever said that, or ever will. Great books don't compete with each other, and neither do great writers.

If you're really committed to studying writing, publishing and marketing, no one will be able to stop you from succeeding. There is no competition for great books, because great books are unique and can't be substituted.

When someone tells you about a great book you have to read, do you ever say, "Oh, I don't need that book because I've already read this other book." Everyone knows that a good book is unique, just like a good writer.

INTERRUPTIONS

Interruptions are a challenge for every writer. You're busy writing your next bestseller, in a whirlwind of creativity when someone rudely opens the door and demands your attention. *"What could possibly be important enough to interrupt me while I'm writing the world's greatest vampire romance novel?!"* you think as you realize your latest creative spark has been dowsed by a 100-gallon bucket of interruption water.

Some interruptions are avoidable while others may not be, depending on your living situation. For starters, you ought to turn off your cell phone and disconnect from the internet while you write. That way you won't get any phone calls, text messages or instant messages interrupting you in the middle of an important writing session (every writing session is important!).

Other interruptions from family members might be a little harder to avoid, but you ought to be proactive about it and prevent interruptions before they occur. You can do that by sitting down with anyone who lives with you and letting them know that when the door is closed in your office/writing space, you are not to be interrupted for any reason except during an emergency.

If you have young children, you might just have to deal with interruptions on a regular basis, but you can definitely reduce the number of interruptions by communicating your need for quiet during your writing time.

Interruptions, like other obstacles to writing success, can be eliminated or at least significantly reduced by being proactive. After the interruption occurs, it's too late to do anything about it!

DISTRACTIONS

Distractions are an entirely different ballgame from interruptions. Interruptions are like someone blowing a whistle while you're trying to shoot a freethrow. Distractions are like walking off the court and missing the game entirely. Where an interruption can ruin one creative writing session, a distraction can ruin hundreds or even thousands of writing sessions.

Distractions threaten your very livelihood as a writer. They will keep you from doing what needs to be done to succeed if you don't deal with them quickly.

Some distractions can't be totally avoided, like when a close family member dies and you must take on new responsibilities for the family. But these distractions are only temporary. Most of us get distracted by shiny new opportunities over and over again, which causes long-term loss of productivity.

Here's how the typical opportunity distraction works: you're thinking about writing one day and you realize it might take you months or even years to earn the kind of money you'd like to as an author. So when you hear about someone getting rich daytrading stocks, you think, *"Aha! My ticket to all the money I could ever dream of. I'll get rich fast and then I can write as much as I want!"* And so you decide to spend 4 hours a day trading instead of writing. Of course, after a few months and a lot of lost money, you decide daytrading really isn't for you and go back to writing.

But then you realize, you're going to need to earn even MORE money now even FASTER to make up for all that lost money from daytrading. So you leap on the next *"get rich quick"* bandwagon, trying to make up lost time from the whole daytrading fiasco. And, of course, that doesn't work out either. That's how most people get stuck in the never-ending cycle of self-sabotage, chasing after all the wrong opportunities.

> ***The best way to make money fast is to focus on becoming really great at something.***

And you can't become really great at something without investing the time. So sit down and write as much as you can, and ignore all distractions that don't have to do with writing, publishing or marketing. Just as jockeys put blinders on their horses so they will look straight ahead, you ought to put blinders on when it comes to writing and ignore all other "opportunities" no matter how much money your uncle Ted made without actually doing any work.

BEING UNKNOWN

The problem with being a new author is that no one knows who you are. But the good news is that no one knows who you are! That means you can write whatever you feel like, and if it turns out to be horrible, at least not many people will know about it. You'll have time to learn and grow and correct your past mistakes.

When I'm speaking to authors about marketing and selling books, I'll always have someone come up to me and ask, "No one knows who I am. So how will I ever become a bestselling author, even if I use these marketing strategies?" It's really a silly question. Every author starts out unknown. If no one has ever heard of you, so what? No one ever heard of Amanda Hocking 10 years ago, and now she's selling hundreds of millions of eBooks.

If you want people to hear about you and know who you are, start writing something worth people talking about. You don't write great books because people talk about you; people talk about you because you write great books (and market them well too).

NOT HAVING CONNECTIONS TO PUBLISHERS, AGENTS OR INDUSTRY INFLUENCERS

Everyone starts off in the publishing industry as a beginner. We were all brand new authors at first, without any connections or relationships with top agents or publishers or movie producers. We all start from ground zero. So if you don't know anyone, that's normal. It's not a bad thing. It's not a negative thing. It's just plain normal—it's how every great author started. Trust me, you're in the right place just where you are. Now it's time to make progress.

If you start writing great books and get published or self-publish them and start marketing your books well, you won't need to chase agents and publishers. They will come to you because they will see how many books you're selling and will want to be on your team. And if you're self-published, you'll probably turn them down knowing that you can earn more as a self-published author earning 100% royalties than as a traditionally published author earning 17% or so.

NOT BEING "GOOD ENOUGH" AT WRITING

If you're not a good writer, you can get better! Writing is a learnable skill, and many who are less intelligent than you have learned to write well. We'll cover writing and how to improve as a writer later on, but for now just realize that we all start out as poor or mediocre writers.

We only get good over time through studying the craft and practicing. So if you're not a good writer, the best place to start is by writing a book! That's the first step to becoming a highly paid author.

CHAPTER 5
THE PUBLISHING REVOLUTION

PUBLISHING IS THE SECOND STEP to becoming a highly paid author, but that's not how most writers see it! Most writers see publishing as the final goal. *"Once I get my book published, I'll have it made!"* is a fantasy that far too many writers delude themselves into believing.

Most traditionally published authors I know earn very little, if anything, from their books. Some earned small advances of a few thousand dollars, while others received even larger advances. The vast majority of them never received a royalty payment because the book sales weren't big enough to earn royalties above and beyond the advance.

Marketing is the third step to becoming a highly paid writer, and because most authors don't even understand this step exists, or act as if they don't, they never sell enough books to earn a substantial income.

If you bought this book hoping you would learn how to get your book published, you're in luck! But, if you bought this book hoping you would learn how to get published, and that would solve all your problems, you're in for a rude awakening.

In the old days, everyone knew what you meant when you said "my book is published." Today, that could mean many, many different things. Is your book published by a Big Six publisher, a traditional publisher, an ebook-only publisher, a small independent publisher, a self-publishing firm, or something else? Did you self-publish it? Is it published as a paperback, hardcover, ebook, audiobook, or app? Is it distributed through Amazon, iBooks, Barnes & Noble, Kobo, Smashwords, or one of the thousands of other book distributors?

The options for publishing today are too many to count. Because the publishing industry has changed so drastically over the last few years, most writers are still struggling just to understand what publishing is anymore. Well, I can tell you one thing—it's not what it used to be!

A few years ago, everyone was talking about the differences between self-publishing and traditional publishing. But even in the last few years, the changes in the industry have been astronomical. There are more self-publishing options today than there have ever been before. And there are more distribution channels for books than there ever have been before, and most of the books now sold are sold through distribution channels that didn't even exist 10 years ago. Add to that the fact that ebooks now outsell physical books by over 30% and you begin to realize just how drastic the changes in the industry have been.

But even though these changes have come so quickly to the publishing industry, the perception of most writers hasn't changed at all. Most writers I talk to today have a simple plan: spend a few years writing a book and then get it published by a traditional publisher and live happily ever after.

Do I believe Tom? I've got old floors!

> *The problem with this plan is that the odds of being successful with this outdated strategy are lower than the odds of winning the lottery!*

Here's why...

First of all, the number of new authors becoming traditionally published has been in decline for several years. Secondly, if you're lucky enough to get a publishing contract today, chances are you will never earn out your advance—meaning you won't ever actually earn any money other than your advance. And third, if you spend a few years writing your book, who knows what the industry will be like by the time you're ready to get published?

At the rate things are changing now, chances are that in 5 years traditional publishing as we know it won't even exist. By 2016, Pricewaterhouse Coopers projects[3] that consumers will spend more money on ebooks than physical books. Today, consumers already purchase more ebooks than physical books, but since ebooks are much cheaper, consumers are still spending more dollars overall on physical books, but not for long.

Question: What will a traditional publisher even do in a world where physical books are only a tiny fraction of overall book sales?

Answer: Publishers will become printers who have relationships with distributors, a shell of what once was the centerpiece of the publishing industry.

So instead of focusing on the differences between traditional publishing vs. self-publishing, an outdated dichotomoy of the industry today, I'd like to share with you the various pieces of the publishing puzzle and how they fit together so that you can:

1) Understand the publishing environment as it is today.

2) Determine which of the many publishing opportunities are right for you.

3) Understand the costs and benefits of various publishing routes.

4) Understand how and why the industry is changing so fast—and where it's headed.

---

[3] http://paidcontent.org/2012/06/12/what-will-the-global-e-book-market-look-like-by-2016/

What Publishing Is

Publishing today can mean many different things. First of all, the question you must ask is, "What kind of book do I want to publish?"

There are dozens of book forms that can be published including paperback books, hardcover books, eBooks, audiobooks, and specialty books (like pop-up books).

Publishing Industry Data

It's very hard—no, impossible—to find perfectly accurate data for book sales. I've done the research and pieced together data from different sources to try to give you the big picture of what's happening now in the industry, where we've been heading and where we're likely to end up in the future.

Please realize that all this data is biased, and none of it should be seen as "the truth". But it is the best data there is, and the picture of what's happening in the industry is quite clear if you learn how to read the data.

In 2011[4], according to Pricewaterhouse Coopers, the Total United States Consumer book market was $19.5 billion (**note**: different sources, such as AAP, will quote very different dollar values of the book market based on the limited data they're reporting. The real number of the U.S. market is close to $20 billion). That number is expected to grow to $21 billion by 2016. That's about a 1.1% annual growth rate, which is actually a negative *real* growth rate when you take into account inflation, which is much higher than 1.1%.

So what does this data show us? First of all, this data shows us that the US consumer book market is very big—$20 billion is a lot of money. Secondly, it shows us that the market is actually *declining*.

---

[4] http://paidcontent.org/2012/06/12/what-will-the-global-e-book-market-look-like-by-2016/

Even though the market is growing by a nominal 1.1% a year, the real growth rate is actually negative when inflation is taken into account. This means consumers are spending slightly less *value* each year on books. I use value here instead of money because consumers are spending more dollars on books each year but the dollars are worth less due to inflation.

According to AAP[5], eBooks accounted for about 22% of all book sales dollars in 2012. AAP reported that the eBook market in 2012 grew by 46% in the US and 44% in the UK.

AAP state that the US downloadable audiobook market in 2012 was $87 million, and grew at a rate of 20-30% annually. So downloadable eBooks make up about 1% of the total US book market.

I created a pie chart based on these numbers that you can see below to get a visual representation for the current book market in 2013, and what the market is projected to be like in 2016. Study these charts well because they may hold the key to your financial future as an author.

ESTIMATED CHART OF US BOOK MARKET 2013

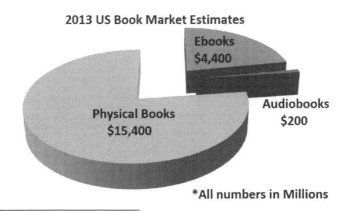

2013 US Book Market Estimates

Ebooks
$4,400

Physical Books
$15,400

Audiobooks
$200

*All numbers in Millions

---

5 http://stephenslighthouse.com/2013/03/03/aap-reports-us-ebook-sales-up-46-in-2012-now-well-over-a-fifth-of-us-book-market/

Projected Chart of US Book Market 2016

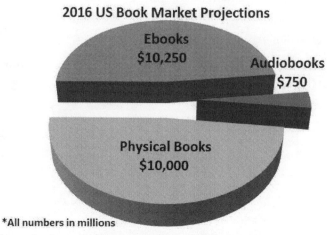

2016 US Book Market Projections

Ebooks
$10,250

Audiobooks
$750

Physical Books
$10,000

*All numbers in millions

Based on the best data we have, you can see that the ebook market is about to grow over the next 3 years from $4.4 billion to over $10 billion, the physical book market is about to shrink from over $15.4 billion to $10 billion, and audiobooks will grow from $200 million to over $750 million.

Of course, all this data is really just a best guess from some of the best financial minds in the world, and no one can truly predict the future. So the numbers could vary significantly. But my best guess is that the ebook market will be between $9-$12 billion, physical books will be $8-$10 billion, and audiobooks will be $400 million to $2 billion (I believe audiobook sales will grow much faster over the next few years than the experts project due to innovations in audiobook technology that will make it easier than ever to create, purchase and listen to audiobooks.)

Regardless of how accurate the actual numbers are, everyone who knows anything about industry sales figures knows three things for sure about the short-term future:

1) Ebook sales will **increase** dramatically
2) Audiobook sales will **increase** dramatically
3) Physical book sales will **decrease** dramatically

And even though we've only discussed the US market here, the same holds true for every other major book market in the world—the UK, Europe, Asia and South America. Ebook and audiobook sales will continue to grow rapidly while physical book sales will continue to decline rapidly.

So what does all this mean for authors like you and me? It means one thing for sure: *if you're hoping to earn a living selling physical books through the old and outdated traditional publishing system, your chances of success are poorer than ever before and getting worse every day!*

On the other hand, *if you plan on selling eBooks over the next few years, your chances of joining the huge pool of authors who are earning a significant income selling ebooks is increasing every day.*

As they say, "a rising tide floats all boats." And trust me when I tell you that the tide of ebook sales has only just begun, and will continue to rise rapidly to the tune of $10 billion a year in US sales by 2016.

But it's not just what readers are buying that's changing the financial future of the industry for authors. There are massive changes just as significant that effect how royalties are paid to authors like you and me!

How Authors Get Paid

In the old days with a traditional publisher, here's how authors got paid:

1) Advance.
2) Royalties.

Advances ranged from $1,000 to several million dollars (reserved only for the few elite with millions of followers). Royalties vary, but generally an author can expect to earn $2 per hardcover and $1 per physical book sold from a traditional publisher (7% to 15%).

Now that eBooks have taken off and will soon surpass physical book sales in total dollar value, everything has changed! EBook distributors such as Amazon.com, Kobo, iBooks, Barnes & Nobles and others now take a cut for each eBook sold ranging from 20% to 65%, depending on the distributor and the price of the book. This means the publisher is earning 35% to 80% royalties on the retail price of the book.

Since Amazon sells over 62% of eBooks currently, you will definitely want your eBook sold on Amazon's Kindle platform. On Amazon, the publisher earns 70% royalties on books priced from $2.99 to $9.99 and 35% royalties for books below $2.99 or above $9.99. This royalty structure highly favors eBooks priced from $2.99 to $9.99—the price range where the publisher and author will earn the most royalties.

If you self-publish your book as an eBook on Amazon Kindle and price it at $2.99, you'll be paid about $2.06 per sale, depending on the delivery costs which are determined by the size of the eBook file. Generally, books with lots of pictures will have higher delivery costs. Books without pictures will often incur 3 cents or less for delivery costs.

So, as a self-published Kindle book author, you would be earning more royalties from selling a $2.99 book than you would as a traditionally published author selling a $24.99 hardcover book!

Of course, $2.99 is not the maximum price for eBooks—you can charge up to $9.99 where you would be earning about $7 in royalties for every sale, a significant raise compared to traditional publishing.

HOW READERS SHOP FOR EBOOKS

Readers shop for books today in a completely different way than they did just a few years ago. In the past, readers would have to hear about a book on TV, the radio, in a newspaper or from a friend. Then, they would go to a bookstore and find the book. Some rare book lovers would wander aimlessly around a bookstore until they found something that caught their eye and they might buy it.

Today, the vast majority of ebooks are not bought because someone heard of it in the media. Most ebooks are bought because someone has a Kindle or other reading device and they start browsing the online store for some good books to download. Word of mouth is still a huge factor in ebook sales, but search is the most important and easily controllable method of finding new readers for new authors without an established platform.

Every day, hundreds of people type in "weight loss" or "paranormal romance" or other similar search phrases in the Kindle store. If you can learn how to rank your books well for keywords that relate to the book using some basic search engine optimization (SEO), you'll sell a lot more books. You don't need a big publisher or a huge marketing budget to do that. You just need learn a little bit about SEO and apply that knowledge to your Kindle book listing. I share all my advanced Amazon SEO strategies for getting search traffic and sales in my previous book *The Kindle Publishing Bible*[6].

But online search isn't the only thing that's changed with how readers find and buy ebooks. Since most ebooks are priced far less than physical books, readers also now buy many more books, and they read much more too. Jeff Bezos announced in 2012[7] that Kindle owners read four times as much as customers who don't own Kindles.

---

[6] http://amzn.to/VNrYLM

[7] http://www.forbes.com/sites/kellyclay/2012/10/12/amazon-confirms-it-makes-no-profit-on-kindles/

Since readers are reading so much more now and buying so many more books, they are willing to try out new authors and, if they find a new author they like, they're much more likely to purchase other books by the same author.

This is why one of the best marketing strategies is simply to write more books. When readers buy one of your books and enjoy it, they're very likely to buy more of your books. That's how you build an author platform—without wasting hours and hours on forums, social media or trying to get your neighbors to buy your book.

The playing field has been completely leveled so to speak. When a customer goes to Amazon.com to browse books or searches for ebooks with their Kindle device, there's absolutely no differentiation between books published by a Big Six publisher and self-published or independently published books. Every listing on Amazon and every other ebook store looks exactly the same! There's no big banner that says, "This book is special because it's published by a big publisher". And anyone, anywhere in the world can publish their books on Amazon, Barnes & Noble, iTunes, Kobo, Smashwords, and elsewhere. That makes it easier than ever for authors to get published and attract new readers.

The playing field hasn't just been leveled, it's been entirely renovated! The way readers find and buy books has changed so much that most authors have been caught offguard. Many still use the old strategies for writing, publishing and marketing, many of which no longer work. So let's talk about some new strategies that work *right now* for creating long-term success.

Chapter 6
New Strategies For A New Age of Publishing

I T'S PRETTY MUCH IMPOSSIBLE TO compare publishing today with how things used to work. You could say, "Publishing today is like it used to be, except instead of selling physical books, more readers are now buying eBooks, and instead of publishers publishing the books, there are more self-publishers now... oh, and everything else is different too!"

Now, because publishing has changed so much and in so many ways, I'm going to be sharing with you some "new" strategies that you've probably never heard of before. These are strategies which would never have been considered under the old publishing model simply because they would not have worked then and any author using these strategies back then would have failed miserably and embarrassed themselves in the process.

In short, it would have been a colossal mistake to use these strategies just a few years ago. But yesterday's colossal mistakes are now today's hottest new strategies for success. So if you find the following strategies to be disgraceful, ridiculous or illegitimate, I would simply ask you to reconsider your thinking - is it ridiculous based on how the industry works *now* or based on *how the industry used to work?*

The Biggest Change of All—Speed

The biggest change with the shift toward eBooks and digital content is that it can be changed almost instantly. If you have a Kindle eBook published and find a typo, you can open up your eBook file, fix the typo, re-upload it to Amazon and, within a few hours, that old version of your book with a typo doesn't exist anymore.

Do you understand how truly incredible and game-changing this one little feature of publishing is? In the old days, if a publisher printed 20,000 books and then you found a typo or an error, there's NOTHING you could do until you printed the next run of another 20,000 books after the first 20,000 had been sold. And do you know how much it would cost just to fix a few typos for a traditional print run? As I said before, the industry is just like it used to be except everything is different!

Because digital content can be changed and updated almost instantaneously, the game has changed.

> *Speed is now more important*
> *than perfection.*

Write that down!

Let me give you an example:

Imagine two authors each write a book about Facebook. They are tutorial books so they have screenshots and show you walkthroughs of how to use Facebook so that people like my Grandma can learn how to use Facebook too. What amazing authors!

Author A is an incredibly skilled writer and a perfectionist who goes by the old model of publishing. He takes two years to write and publish the book, and it's ABSOLUTELY PERFECT! There are no typos and every factual tidbit in the book is 100% accurate. It is literally a perfect book.

Author B is a good writer, but not incredible by any means. He's not a perfectionist either, he just wants to write a book that's "good enough." So he writes his book on Facebook in four months and publishes it. It's far from perfect! His first readers tell him about a dozen typos and factual errors. So what does he do? He takes that feedback and fixes all the errors and typos, and in a few hours they don't exist anymore. In a few weeks, his book only has a few typos left and is now totally factually accurate, thanks to some helpful feedback from readers.

At first, Author A sells more books than Author B because it has more 5-star reviews and readers know it's a really well-written book. Then Facebook makes some changes. They release Timeline and Facebook Offers and all kinds of other changes. Author B, being proactive, updates his book to reflect these new changes and in a few hours those updates are now live. Author B's new readers now start leaving 5-star reviews, impressed that the book has such up-to-date information. Author A's book starts getting more and more negative reviews as readers realize that the content is out of date. Eventually, Author A's sales dry up while Author B takes over the market because his book is so up to date.

Do you understand now why speed is more important than perfection? Everyone talks about how the world is changing faster than ever, and how "the world is flat." Why then do so many authors take so long to embrace these crucial changes?

But it's not just the speed at which you make updates to your books that will give you a competitive advantage; it can also be speed to market, or how fast you publish. Assuming Author A and Author B had started writing at the same time, Author B would have had a year and eight months head start on sales. You can sell a lot of books in a year and eight months! And you can build an incredible author brand in that time as well.

Publishing fast provides a huge advantage. Yes, there are downsides to it. Your book might have mistakes in it. It might not be perfect. People might leave bad reviews. But your book is going to get bad reviews anyways, assuming it has any modicum of success. Harry Potter has

Eighty-eight 1-star reviews last time I checked. So you'll be in good company.

Now, I know that publishing your books quickly might sound like taking the easy way out. It kind of sounds like taking a shortcut. But I'm telling you that it's in your best interest financially to do so. I'm not saying you should publish your book before it's done and then never fix or update it. You should constantly be improving your books whether they are published or unpublished!

This strategy of publishing quickly will only work for you if you're willing to do the extra work it requires to fix all your mistakes as quickly as possible. Otherwise, this strategy will backfire. But, if you want to become a highly paid author, this is a strategy that's worked very well for me and many other highly paid authors who sell a lot of eBooks.

Look at author Steve Scott as an example. He published his first Kindle book in February, 2012. Today, he has 14 published books on Kindle and is consistently ranked in the Top 100 Business & Investing authors on Amazon. I've talked to Steve personally and even interviewed him about his success[8], and he's just a regular, down-to-Earth kind of guy who understands that writing great books and publishing quickly is a great strategy for success today.

Short Books vs. Long Books

In the past, books were expected to be long. The longer, the better. Today, we live in a fast-paced world where people can't wait in an elevator for 10 seconds without checking their smartphones (hey, maybe they're reading your book while they wait 10 seconds!). Because we live in such a fast-paced society, you might want to consider using this trend to your advantage by writing shorter books.

---

[8] http://www.youtube.com/watch?v=0GHrsPCvKfs

Now, this only really applies to non-fiction authors. For you fiction writers, writing good sized novels from 80,000 to 120,000 words or so is going to be the best strategy for becoming a highly paid author. People aren't willing to pay $2.99 or more for a 10,000 word short story, because in 20 minutes they'll be done with it and bored already.

Fiction writers, even though your book will be long, it should *read quickly*. That means it must be a fast-paced novel. Right from the beginning, the book should draw the reader into the story. There shouldn't be long, boring back-story for page after page, because no one wants that. We want dialogue, we want action, we want something that will instantly whisk us away to a new experience!

Although you probably won't be writing a short eBook, it should *feel short*. After spending several hours reading your book, it should feel like it was only a few minutes. If you can do that, readers will devour every novel you write.

For you non-fiction writers, on the other hand, shorter really is better. If you're anything like me and you've ever read a 300+ page non-fiction book and afterwards not remembered a damn thing, then you know what I mean. Some authors just go on and on endlessly about the same topic, including minute details that no one cares about except academics or geniuses or someone with nothing better to do than use a dictionary to look up every other archaic word. Don't treat your readers like that!

No one wants to read an academic text book except, well, academics. But most non-fiction books these day sound academic. In other words, they're frickin' boring! Don't bore your readers to death. When you've finished making a point, move on. And don't share irrelevant facts, details or anecdotes about your dog Fluffy. Keep your writing relevant.

A non-fiction book should clearly address, describe and solve a problem for the reader. For example, if you're writing a book about stress, your book should clearly explain the problem and one or multiple solutions for solving the problem. You don't need to write a 732-page book on stress. Get to the point!

Readers with a stress problem really don't care about all the studies on stress or the history of the science on stress; all they want to know is how to fix their problem. The quicker and more effectively you provide the solution, the more readers will love you.

And, the more books you'll be able to write, because instead of one 700-page book on stress, you could write ten 70-page books on different stress-related issues like stress relief, panic attacks, anxiety, fear, anger, etc. And if you have ten published, focused books, you'll probably sell more than ten times as many books because each book will be attracting new readers to your brand and helping you build your author platform.

In short, write shorter non-fiction books and get to the point. Most eBook readers don't appreciate long non-fiction books with few insightful ideas.

GET PERSONAL

For non-fiction writers, I know it may sound strange and unprofessional, but I believe you should get more personal with your writing. Instead of writing "The author remembers growing up...", you should just write, "I remember growing up..."

Human beings crave personal connection, and they will relate to you better and connect with you more if you use personal language rather than abstractions and impersonal words.

In addition to writing "I", you ought to use "you" as much as possible instead of using impersonal language. Here's an example.

Impersonal and Boring Language: "Authors would sell more books if they used personal language."

Personal, Engaging Language: "You will sell more books if you use personal language."

I know, it sounds so simple. And it is simple. But it will make a big difference in how readers relate to you. If you use personal language, readers will feel like they know you more intimately. And people who know you better tend to like you more. And people who like you more are more willing to buy from you.

All great marketers understand this principle and have used it to sell a lot of products. Look at billboards or advertisements on TV or any other form of media or advertising—using personal language is what grabs people's attention and holds their attention.

The same holds true for readers. Don't bore me by talking about other people—talk about me! If you talk about me, I'll probably pay attention. If you use impersonal nouns like "authors" as the subject of all your sentences and write boring sentences like "one should remember to always write as if one was not a real person and was rather a writing robot", you're not going to hold the reader's attention as well as you could.

Keep your writing conversational. It's a lot less boring, don't you think?

The Ultimate Author Marketing Strategy

In addition to writing books, I highly recommend creating other valuable content for your audience. After working with dozens of other bestselling authors as a publisher and marketing consultant, I've developed what I call The Ultimate Author Marketing Strategy based on what's worked for myself and so many other bestselling authors.

This is the strategy almost every bestselling self-published and indie author used to become so successful.

First, I must warn you because this strategy is so incredibly simple that it might seem "too easy" or "too obvious". I would urge you to set aside such notions and first seek to fully understand the strategy, and then apply it and test it for yourself. You will be amazed by the results you see even though the strategy is so very simple.

CREATE MASSIVELY VALUABLE CONTENT REGULARLY FOR YOUR AUDIENCE

The key foundation to the Ultimate Author Marketing Strategy is that you must create massively valuable content regularly for your audience. There are many, many ways you can do so, but any method will work as long as you follow the three key principles of this approach:

1) PROVIDE MASSIVE VALUE

We're not talking about a little bit of value—we're talking about MASSIVE value. Massive value means that your content actually *makes a difference* in someone's life. After indulging in your incredible content, your audience should feel inspired, educated, or thoroughly entertained. They should remember that experience for days, weeks, months and even years to come. It should be an emotional and not just an intellectual experience for greatest effect.

2) PROVIDE VALUE REGULARLY

It's not just enough to give people a wonderful book or a wonderfully entertaining video once. You must be *regularly* providing amazingly valuable content for your audience. "Regularly" should be at a MINIMUM weekly for most forms of content, but it might be daily or monthly depending on how easily and quickly it can be produced. For example, blog posts and short videos can be created much more quickly than hour-long videos with special effects and entire books.

3) CREATE VALUE FOR YOUR AUDIENCE

Finally, you must create this incredible value for *your* audience—not random people who may or may not even care about your books or what you do. You want to create massive value for your audience who will be likely to purchase your books and share them with others. Realize that you must focus on helping *one* audience.

Don't try to be everything to everyone—focus on one audience, write books in one niche or genre, and do everything you can to help that one audience. That's how you create an author platform and a real business, because everyone in that audience will come to know you through your extensive volume of helpful and interesting content.

For example, if you write about business, you ought to be creating content that is interesting and valuable to people interested in business. If you write young romance novels, you ought to be creating content that's valuable and interesting to people who read young romance novels. Writing romance novels and creating educational videos about business will not help you become a bestselling novelist because you're trying to cater to multiple audiences. Make sure your value is a match for your audience and only create content for your one audience!

CONTENT CREATION OPTIONS

There are many, many kinds of content you can create and even more ways to distribute this content to your audience. *The key is to pick one kind of content and only one distribution strategy and become the absolute master of that channel, giving your audience massive value consistently.*

KINDS OF CONTENT

- ❖ *Written Word*
- ❖ *Audio*

❖ *Pictures / Visual*
❖ *Video*

All of these forms of content can be used, but you ought to focus on just one form of content and become the master in that arena.

Distribution Channels

The major distribution channels today in order of importance are:

1) YouTube

I believe YouTube is the most important channel because video is the most powerful form of content, and YouTube is the largest video distribution channel in the world. Video is much more interactive and personal than written text, pictures or even audio. Video communicates using both the visual and auditory centers of your audience's brain and will hold their attention better and allow you to convey even more information and entertainment in less time.

You can even use YouTube videos to add more value to your books. If you're writing about a particular process, why not create a video tutorial that walks readers through that process as well? This is a great way to add more value, connect more deeply with your readers and set yourself apart from others in your niche or genre.

A great example of someone creating amazing content and an entire business based only on YouTube marketing is Luxy Hair[9] created by Mimi. Luxy Hair has over 132 million views on YouTube and almost 1 Million subscribers. YouTube is the only platform they use to distribute their educational content which has helped her create a massive online business.

Remember what I said before – just focus on becoming a master in one platform!

---

[9] http://www.youtube.com/user/LuxyHair

2) FACEBOOK

Facebook is incredibly powerful because it is the largest website in the world—over 1 billion people use Facebook regularly, and Facebook Fan Pages were created so that people like you can build an audience and stay in touch with them daily. This creates the opportunity for some incredibly powerful ongoing relationship building and marketing if done well.

Drew Canole's Facebook Page Juicing Vegetables[10] is a great example of someone who's created a massive online brand using Facebook. Drew's page has over 560,000 Facebook fans and it's helped propel his book Juicing Recipes from FitLife[11] to a #1 bestseller on Amazon with over 500 reviews averaging 4.5 stars and consistently ranked as one of the top 2,500 bestselling books on Kindle. How did he do it? He focused 100% on building his platform on Facebook!

3) BLOGGING

Blogging is incredibly powerful as well. It takes a lot more work than many other content distribution strategies simply because there are a lot of technical aspects you must understand far beyond simply writing blog posts, but if you're up for learning it can be incredibly rewarding. You can also create video posts for your blog as well as text posts.

Tim Ferriss is a great example of someone who's become a #1 New York Times bestselling author and built a massive platform and online business almost entirely through blogging. Tim's blog[12] is consistently ranked one of the top 25 blogs in the world. How did he do it? He focused 100% on blogging and provides the most incredibly valuable content and information on his blog that he possibly can. He also

---

[10] https://www.facebook.com/VegetableJuicing
[11] http://www.amazon.com/dp/B007DDQYCU/
[12] http://www.fourhourworkweek.com/blog/

studied blog design and marketing intensely, and of course applies what he learns.

See Tim's video on How to Blog without Killing Yourself[13] to learn more.

4) PODCASTING

Podcast shows are incredibly powerful, and many completely unknown people have become "famous" simply by creating an amazingly valuable podcast show. Podcast shows can be either audio or video or a mix, and your audience will download your shows from either iTunes or a website online.

Abel James is a great example of someone absolutely dominating in the podcasting platform. Abel's show Fat Burning Man[14] reached the #2 podcast spot on iTunes just behind Jillian Michaels – and a year before that no one had ever heard of Abel or his podcast show. How did he do it? He focused ONLY on podcasting and created the best content he could.

5) TWITTER

Twitter is a powerful channel with hundreds of millions of active users, but it can be very limiting and it's difficult to build a large Twitter following without using at least one other content channel such as those listed above. I wouldn't recommend focusing on Twitter unless you enjoy being incredibly social online.

Gary Vaynerchuk[15] is a great example of someone who's absolutely crushing it on Twitter and has built a massive following of raving fans. Gary is very active on Twitter and is brilliant when it comes to social media and how to build long-term relationships with customers and

---

[13] http://www.fourhourworkweek.com/blog/2009/06/29/how-to-build-a-high-traffic-blog-without-killing-yourself/

[14] http://www.fatburningman.com/

[15] https://twitter.com/garyvee

followers. Always remember – long-term relationships lead to long-term success!

IMPLEMENTING THE ULTIMATE AUTHOR MARKETING STRATEGY

Now that you understand the foundation of this life-changing strategy and what channels you can use, let's talk about implementation—here's what you must DO in order to make this strategy work for you and create a lifelong income from royalties that would make your mother blush.

PICK ONE CHANNEL AND MASTER IT

You must first pick only ONE channel and then master it. Don't try to be a Facebook, Twitter, Blogging, Podcasting and YouTube master. Just focus on ONE strategy and become the best you can be at that strategy. Splitting your attention, focus and content amongst different channels will only dilute your message and reduce your value in the marketplace, thus reducing your income!

Instead, focus on increasing your value by becoming a master in your one channel. It's a good idea to have a profile set up for Twitter, Facebook, YouTube, and other major social networks and channels, but you should focus on creating massive value in one area so that you're not spreading your daily energy and effort too thinly.

For fiction authors, I recommend using either Facebook or Blogging. John Locke credits blogging as one of the keys to his success in selling over 1 million eBooks. And Facebook is a great way to connect with your audience on a more personal level than you can through your books.

For non-fiction authors, I recommend YouTube or Facebook. YouTube will provide the most in-depth engagement with your audience and help you provide a ton of value and get a lot of traffic and sales for your books over time.

MASTERY MUST BE PRACTICED DAILY

In order to become a true master, you must practice daily! I recommend spending 30 minutes a day creating content for your channel. You don't have to do exactly 30 minutes a day; you could spend 3.5 hours one day a week and then schedule your content to be released each day over the week. Every week at a minimum you should have new content for your audience.

The key here is regularity and consistency! That's why this strategy is so simple—anyone can spend 30 minutes a day creating a video or writing a blog post.

The reason 99% of people fail to become successful as bloggers or YouTubers is because they are not providing massive value regularly. They create a few videos a week for a few weeks and then take a few months off. They're not 100% committed to their success.

If you are 100% committed to your success, you will work daily to achieve your goals and you will succeed. If you are 99% committed to your success, you will fail.

If you start creating great content in one of these channels regularly, you probably won't see any significant results for the first 3-6 months. But between 6 months and a few years, the results you see will be astronomical. Your success will look like a typical exponential equation graph—progress at first will seem miniscule, but after a while the exponential effects kick in and book sales grow at incredible rates.

That's exactly what happened to me and every other successful author I know. For several months or years, sales grew steadily or very slowly if at all. Then, all of a sudden sales take off and you go from a few sales a month to a few thousand sales a month. It looks like overnight success to the outside world, but it's the exponential growth kicking in from months and years of effort and intelligent work.

People will ask, "How did you become a #1 bestselling author?" and "How did you get millions of YouTube views?" and "How did you get tens of thousands of Facebook fans?" When you are asked these questions about your incredible success, you'll know that it's because you put in the time, the effort, and the energy.

There was little luck involved; it just took time for the exponential effect to kick in.

Chapter 7
Your Daily Method of Operation

WHEN I WAS 19 YEARS old, I attended a weekend retreat in Traverse City, Michigan put on by a network marketing company. At the retreat, there were dozens of speakers who were sharing their "keys to success" in the business and direct sales world.

One of the speakers in particular really got my attention when he was teaching. His name was Jeff Roberti, and he's earned over $100 million in commissions and sold billions of dollars of products in the network marketing industry . He's one of the top producers in the industry, and his success is absolutely incredible.

Jeff said that his Daily Method of Operation (DMO) is what made him so successful. Now, everyone in the network marketing industry knows that the key to success is to sell products and recruit new distributors. And everyone knows that if you talk to more people, you will make more sales. It's common sense. It's obvious! Everyone knows that's how you maximize your income. Likewise, all writers know that the more books you write and the more promotion you do, the more money you will earn.

Jeff said the problem isn't that people don't know what to do to earn more money—the problem is that they don't do what they know they should do. It's really easy to sit down for two hours and write. But what's easy to do is also easy not to do. It's easy to watch TV, play video games or chat with friends instead of sitting down and writing. It's easier to complain about how bad business is than it is to get to work and make your business better.

This problem of not doing what we know we should do plagues all of us if we don't destroy it. It's like a virus that slowly drains you of your energy and success if you don't take drastic measures to kill this bad habit once and for all. And the only way to do that is by creating a successful DMO and sticking to it.

Your DMO is like a daily ritual for your work. It's something you must first create for yourself, write down on paper, and then do every single day to turn your dreams into a reality. Your DMO is what will determine your success or failure. The truth is, we all have a DMO; some of us have just put more time, effort and energy into planning our DMO than others. Most writers simply live their day by default. Instead of actively planning their days for success, they fall into old habits that lead to failure or mediocrity. And there's nothing wrong with that. It's okay to live a mediocre life if that's all you want. But if you want to be a highly paid author, you absolutely must have a successful DMO.

Jeff's Daily Method of Operation when he first started his network marketing business was absolutely incredible, especially when you compare it to the average distributor. When most of the top people in the company, the ones earning $10,000 a month or more, were talking to 5 to 10 new prospects a day, Jeff was talking to 100 or more prospects a day. He worked 16 hours a day on the phone, talking to people in person, or speaking on stages and at events. Every single week, Jeff would talk to at least 700 people about his business. In one year, that's over 35,000 people. But he didn't just do that for one year—he kept up that level of activity for 5 years. That's over 175,000 people he talked to! And now he earns millions of dollars a year because of the work he did during those 5 years. Your next 5 years could be just as life-changing for you if you commit to taking advantage of the opportunity you have today.

Now let me ask you a question—if you talked to 175,000 people about your book, do you think you would sell some copies? Of course you would! Now I'm not telling you that the fastest or easiest path to success is to start talking to 100 people a day about your book. What I'm trying to show you is the power of a strong DMO. Many people say that "success is a numbers game," and it is! Remember the 10,000 hours it takes to become a master at something? Guess what, it's a numbers game—the more time you practice writing, the better you will be. And the ONLY WAY to get in enough hours to create the kind of success you want is to create a DMO that will get you there. Otherwise, you're just hoping to get lucky.

CREATING YOUR DMO FOR SUCCESS

So what should a highly paid writer's DMO look like? Here's what I believe is the minimal DMO for a highly paid writer. The numbers I'm about to share with you are the minimum for what you ought to do to become a highly paid writer. If you do more, you will only become successful even faster. If you do less, you may still become a highly paid writer but it will take much longer unless you get very lucky.

Writing:

2 hours a day, 7 days a week (or at least 15 hours a week).

Editing:

As needed.

Studying:

Studying writing, publishing, marketing and other areas necessary to improve your skills and sales.

Reading:

All great writers are voracious readers. Every day you should be filling your mind with great words and great ideas from other great writers.

Notebooking:

Notebooking is a word I made up for writing notes in my notebook such as to-do lists, book ideas, brainstorming, asking myself questions, reflecting, journaling, etc. If you could only develop one daily habit to lead you to success other than writing, notebooking should be it because it's the fastest path to learning new things and solving your current problems.

Eating healthy food:

Your success as a writer depends on your brain's ability to function. If you're eating unhealthy, greasy processed foods and fast food, you're lowering circulation to your brain and it's been proven that unhealthy diets lower mental performance. How do you expect to become a master writer with impaired mental activity? If you eat healthy food, you will write better, feel better and be more successful. You'll probably live longer too so you can enjoy your big royalty checks for a few more years hopefully.

Exercise:

This is important for the same reason eating healthy food is. Your health is vital to your success, and we all know exercise is important for our health. For writers, exercise can also be a fantastic way to clear your mind and create new ideas. I often find fantastic ideas come to me when I'm exercising. Just remember to keep your notebook or smartphone nearby so you can jot down those great ideas!

Resting:

Take time off to rest, reflect and be creative. Working consistently and persistently is important, but you still need to take time off for rest and relaxation to unleash your full creative potential.

Marketing:

 Apply the Ultimate Author Marketing Strategy every day.

A LITTLE EXPLANATION

To clarify some points about the DMO above...

Writing time means time spent writing—physically typing keys on your keyboard or writing with pen and paper. Thinking about writing, sitting at your computer without typing, or anything else is NOT writing. You must actually produce new words and ideas when you write—otherwise, it's not writing, is it?

Editing time should never compete with writing time. What I mean is, you should always be writing new material at your DMO rate. So if you're done writing your first book and you're now editing that book, you should immediately start writing your second book at the DMO rate while you edit the first book. This is crucial for many, many reasons. In network marketing, many would-be successful distributors get stuck in "management mode." Management mode is when you stop doing what made you successful and start trying to manage your team instead of going out and making new sales.

Many writers make the same mistake—they stop writing new material and focus for months or years on editing old material. That's a big mistake! If you're not writing new material, then you're not producing any new books. That means you're not making anything new that will make you more money. Is it important to edit your books? Absolutely. But it's also important that you keep creating new material so that you can get paid. Not only does it make good sense financially, but it will make you a far better writer by being disciplined and putting in those extra hours of practice. Remember, editing is not the same as writing.

Another problem with getting into management mode is that it kills your momentum. Momentum is a big key to success that most unsuccessful people don't even know exists. Have you ever known someone who just seemed like they had everything going for them? Maybe they were a fellow author who seemed to be producing a new bestselling book every few months, or maybe they were a businessperson who seemed to always be up to something new. What makes these people so successful? Why does everything seem to be going right for them? The answer is usually momentum.

The fascinating thing about momentum is that you can create positive momentum very quickly and it will always lead to success. In fact, when you start to create that positive momentum, you will have this self-confidence and inner knowing that you will be wildly successful, even before the money comes. I'll never forget when I found my momentum. It started shortly after creating my writing DMO. I was writing several hours a day, recording one video a day to post on YouTube, and I was reading, studying or learning about publishing and marketing books for at least one hour a day.

When I started following my DMO every day, my Kindle royalties at the time were less than $200 a month. I already knew I was going to make it big as an author. I just knew that I was going to be a bestselling author and earning huge royalty checks every month. Some might call it arrogance or overconfidence, but it was just a feeling I had inside with absolute certainty that I was going to be successful. In fact, if you had asked me then, I would have told you that *I already felt successful as an author*—even though I was only earning $200 a month. *I felt so successful even without the money because I was doing everything successful authors do.* There was no doubt in my mind. I was investing the time in writing new books, editing, studying, reading, marketing—everything I needed to do to be successful, I was doing.

Let me ask you this: *if you knew you were doing everything it took to become a successful author, would you feel different? Would you feel more confident, successful and fulfilled? Would there be any doubt in your mind about your inevitable success?*

 The reason most of us struggle and feel unsuccessful is because we know deep down that we're not doing what it takes to create the success we want. We know our DMO is not leading us to where we want to go, either consciously or subconsciously. And that's why we feel so bad about ourselves. It's why we're not confident about our career and our success. But as soon as we create the DMO that will lead us to success, everything changes—immediately! Way before the money comes, you will know you're already successful because you will be doing what it takes to succeed.

There will be no more uncertainty, fear and doubt left in your mind. And when the money does come, you will be grateful and proud. You will know that you truly earned it with all your hard work and effort. You will be living your life by design instead of by default.

Six months after I started my writing DMO, I had my first month where I earned over $10,000 in Kindle royalties alone. Maybe your success will come that quickly and maybe it won't. All I know is that you will be successful if you do what it takes to become successful. I couldn't stop the money from flowing in now if I tried. I have momentum on my side. And even if I stopped writing, I couldn't stop my old books from selling.

Your success will come the same way. You won't be able to stop the money and success from flowing to you if you have the right DMO and you're implementing it every day. Success becomes inevitable when you're doing the right things in the right way every day.

Action Steps

Right now, create your DMO. You can start by writing down what activities you are going to START DOING so that you can achieve the success you want. You don't have to create the perfect DMO right away. The best way to create a great DMO is one step at a time. Start with one new activity that will put you on the path to success, and then add another, and another, and another. Before you know it, success will be knocking on your door.

What Not To Do

We all know that we must do something new to get different results. So we know that writing a few more hours a week will improve our results and output. It's easy to understand, but harder to do.

> *What most of us don't realize, though, is that it's just as important to change what you don't do as it is to change what you do.*

We all have 24 hours a day to get things done. And I know you used all 24 hours of your time yesterday. Whether you used them wisely or not is up to you. But regardless, you used all 24 hours. So if you want to do something different today than what you did yesterday, you're going to have to reduce or eliminate some other activity or behavior that you're used to doing on a regular basis. This means getting rid of old habits.

Let's say that based on your DMO, you need to add in two more hours of writing time every day. That means you must remove two hours of activity (or inactivity) from your old behaviors. It sounds obvious, but most of us don't plan for making changes at this level. And because we only plan new behaviors and don't plan to remove old behaviors to make time, we find ourselves too busy, stressed out and not able to spend as much time on our DMO as we wanted.

Just as you created your DMO of daily activities that you must do, *it's important to create your DMO of daily activities that you must not do.* Jim Rohn said, "if it's not necessary to do, it's necessary not to do." I don't think more wisdom has ever been packed inside such a small sentence. If what's on your DMO list is necessary to achieving the success you want, then everything else is not necessary to achieving that success. Now, there are many, many forms of success beyond becoming a highly paid author. You can achieve relationship success, social success, sports success, personal success, spiritual success, and success in any area of life. I'm not saying you must sacrifice all other forms of success for this one form of financial success as an author. What I'm saying is that you must sacrifice all activities that are not necessary to your success, however you define success for you.

Let's use television as an example. Ever since I was 19, I threw away my TV and stopped watching television altogether. Watching TV was one of those behaviors I put on my "necessary not to do list." Why? Because watching just one hour of TV a day meant 7 hours a week of lost time. After a year, that's 365 hours of lost time—that's over 45 eight-hour work days! Most people wonder why they can't get ahead in life. It's because your competitors gave up an hour a day of TV or something else so that they could have an extra 45 work days of productivity! Imagine what you could do with 45 extra work days per year. Most authors can write a short book or novella in that time, and many can write a full-length novel in less time.

Time is your most precious asset and you must learn to use it even more wisely than you use your money or other possessions.

Looking long-term, you realize that cutting out one hour of TV a day could help you write at least one new book each year. And if that's ALL you did for 20 years, you'd have twenty completed books. So what would you rather have—one hour a day of mediocre entertainment or 20 published books? The choice is yours! You could easily create a full-time income with a portfolio of 20 books, and all it would take is 20 years of 1 hour writing each day instead of 1 hour of watching TV. Looking at things this way, does success really seem all that difficult to come by?

Unfortunately, we were never taught these concepts in school. No one taught us to look long-term at our lives and see how our present behaviors might effect our long-term outcomes. Instead, we're taught to cram for tests so that we can get good grades. We're taught to think short-term effort for short-term rewards. But every great achievement in life doesn't happen in a short period of time! Everything great in life happens over a long-term period of time. It takes day after day after day of writing to complete a book. But since we were taught to focus on short-term results, we try to write a whole book in a day or a week and get upset when it doesn't work out. Or we try to get our book published in one day or a week. Or we try to do all our marketing in one day or a week. The truth is, most people quit before they finish anything great in life. That's why Les Brown says, "the richest place in the world is the graveyard." It's because all those dead people had great ideas for creating wealth and improving the world, but they never finished what they started—and many didn't even start at all!

Don't let that happen to you! If you're serious about achieving success, create your DMO and create your list of behaviors that you must eliminate. Common time-wasters that many people benefit from eliminating include:

- ❖ Watching TV.
- ❖ Watching the news, reading newspapers and online news sites.
- ❖ Surfing the internet.
- ❖ Reading magazines.
- ❖ Checking email over and over.
- ❖ Playing video games and computer games.

In addition to these common areas where many of us waste time, I've found that there are some areas particularly for authors and people who work from home such as:

- ❖ Checking sales reports daily or multiple times a day (if you're self-published).
- ❖ Checking social media accounts multiple times a day.
- ❖ Generally unproductive activity on the computer (it varies from person to person, but it often involves checking particular websites repeatedly).

All of these behaviors have a one thing in common: *they're robbing you of your success!*

Imagine that you have a room in which you can put boxes of particular behaviors. Your room only has 24 hours a day in it. What most of us do is stack up our room with things that aren't all that important until it's totally full. Then, one day we decide we want to be successful and we're going to go for it! So we try to cram in all these new successful activity boxes in our room. There's just one little problem—there's no room! But unlike other rooms, this one is always full. We always use our 24 hours a day. So you must simultaneously remove the old boxes while you put in the new ones. The only way to be successful is to actively engage in new, more effective behaviors while eliminating old, ineffective behaviors.

Realize also that removing an activity doesn't mean that that activity will never get done. For example, you might find it necessary for someone to check your blog for new comments and remove spam comments, but it doesn't have to be YOU doing those activities. You can delegate such activities to your team so that you can focus on high-value activities that will lead you to success. We'll talk about how to create your success team in the next chapter.

ACTION STEPS

Right now, write down what activities you are going to STOP DOING so that you can achieve the success you want.

PLANNING YOUR DAYS IN ADVANCE

Your DMO is your daily plan for success, but there's one small problem with it – it's fixed! Maybe you've created your DMO so that you write at least two hours a day, but now you're on a tight deadline to edit a book for your publisher or maybe it's your spouse's birthday and you're going to take him or her out for a special day. The point is that every day is a different day, and things change. So you must also be flexible and change. There are certain things you must do on certain days that just can't be included in your DMO. That's why you must start the habit of *planning your day in advance.*

Here's how I do it:

Before I go to bed at night, I grab my notebook and I write down everything on my "to do" list. If I have any appointments at certain times, I write those down. If I have any major projects I need to complete, I write that down. Basically, all the important things you need to do to have a successful day. I write this all down and plan for it the night before so that as soon as I wake up, I'm ready to go and start my day on the most important tasks that will help me achieve my goals and dreams. I can't stress how important that is!

Personally, I've found that mornings can be the hardest time to get things done, but the most crucial time to do so. For example, if I wake up late and have to run off to some errand or appointment and don't get any work done in the morning, I often find that I have a very unproductive day. Even if I'm home in the afternoon or evening and can work then, I find I don't get nearly as much done and I just don't feel as productive.

On the other hand, if I wake up early and get some work done in the morning, even if it's only thirty minutes or an hour of work, I find I often have a very productive day. Maybe it's just me, and maybe you will be more productive in the afternoon or evening, but either way planning your day in advance is a powerful tool for creating the success you desire.

Now, once I've planned my day the night before and have my to do list, it's time to prioritize activities. Now there are all kinds of time management systems for prioritizing activities, and some are certainly better than others. Some people recommend grading your list with A's, B's, and C's – A's being the highest priority tasks and C's being the lowest priority. Personally, I find that to be a big waste of time, especially if I have a rather large to do list on a particular day. Instead, I just mark down my *most important task* with a star.

Here's why – everything in life has a priority to you. Some things are more important to you and some things are less important. If you spend your whole life accomplishing less important tasks and skipping out on the most important tasks, you'll live a mediocre life at best, ruled by old habits. But if you accomplish your *most important tasks* in life each day, you'll live an incredibly successful life.

The key is to figure out what's most important *for you*. Once you know what's most important, focus on that task and get it done first thing in the morning. Once you're in the work flow and have accomplished the most important task, it will be a breeze to work through the other items on your to do list.

Personally, this is the system that works best for me. I love it because it ensures I get the most important things done every day, but it takes less than 5 minutes of my time so I'm not investing a lot of energy, effort and time in the process. As Buckminster Fuller said, it's how you "do more with less."

After I'm done with my most important task in the morning, that's when I start to focus on more of my DMO tasks. Sometimes, my most important task is writing a new book. Sometimes it's making a phone call or doing something completely new that I never anticipated. Your most important task each day doesn't necessarily have to be a part of your DMO. But once you accomplish your most important task, it's time to start working on your DMO.

So here's my daily planning process again in simplified form:

CREATING YOUR DAILY PLANNING CHECKLIST

Step 1. Write Down Your To Do List For Tomorrow Before You Go To Bed.

Step 2. Put a star next to your highest priority task.

Step 3. Read your list first thing in the morning and work on your most important task first, only moving on once you've accomplished it.

Step 4. Continue working on your to do list, making sure you're accomplishing what you set out to do in your DMO

Step 5. At night, go over what you accomplished today. Take a few moments to appreciate what you accomplished as you go over the items crossed off on your list, and transfer any remaining items to your list for tomorrow if they're still important.

Step 6. Repeat the process every day

Here's how I look at it: my DMO is my overall plan for daily success. It helps me create a *minimum standard of daily activity* that will help me achieve my goals. But knowing that things change so much from day to do, I use my Daily Planning Checklist to make sure I get done everything that's in my DMO as well as new and important tasks that come up from time to time.

In other words, the Daily Planning Checklist is my daily habit that ensures I accomplish what I set out to do in my DMO – the key activities I know will lead me to success if I only continue to do them daily.

CREATING YOUR MONTHLY METHOD OF ACTION (MMA)

Right now we're going to discuss long-term planning and how to create your MMA—Monthly Method of Action.

Your DMO is the key to becoming successful because it's your *daily* activity that will create progress for your career. You only have today to get things done! Tomorrow never comes and yesterday is gone forever. So focus today on what you can do to improve your life and achieve your goals. The DMO is a tool to help you get more success from each day.

Now, I know, most self-help gurus today would tell you to set your long-term goals first and then set your short-term goals. But setting a DMO isn't about goal-setting, it's about goal-achieving! And there's a huge difference between goal-setting and goal-achieving, a difference which I'm sure you can appreciate assuming you've set goals in the past but failed to achieve them. The difference is always in the daily activity. That's why you ought to first create your daily activity plan.

Chances are *you already have long-term goals*. You want to become a highly paid author? That's a long-term goal, and it's good enough to get you started moving in the right direction. Whether your goal is to earn $100,000 a year in royalties or $1,000,000 a year in royalties really doesn't matter; your daily activity is what will get you to your goal and beyond.

Right now, we're going to talk about long-term planning. Planning and goal-setting are quite different. Planning is focused on activity and goals are focused on results. Set your goals, by all means, but once you have your goals written down, you better have a plan to *achieve your goals,* or else what's the point? Your DMO is your daily plan. Your long-term plan is your MMA. That's right, long-term planning should be *one month away.*

Most people plan far too long in the future. You think, "In 5 years from now, I'll publish my book and become an overnight success." Ha! What are the chances of that happening? Who knows where you'll be 5 years from now? That's a very, very, very long time away. *Most people use long-term planning as an excuse not to get to work today to make their dreams come true.* Instead of setting 5-year goals, set 1-month *plans.* Can you finish that book you're working on in 30 days? If your immediate answer is "no way!" then I would urge you to consider this question:

If you could finish your book in the next 30 days, how would you do it?

Notice that this is a **very different question** from the first one. This question already assumes you can finish your book in 30 days, and it forces you to *plan* your Monthly Method of Action in order to achieve that goal. Now, I know, there may be a million reasons why you can't finish your book in 30 days, or achieve some other seemingly large goal in 30 days. **But there is absolutely no excuse for not trying!**

Let's pretend you're waiting on research results to be finished before you can complete your book. And there's literally no way it could get done in 30 days without an act of God. **That's still no excuse for not trying!**

If you want to be successful, you must do everything in your power to make your dreams come true, and leave the acts of God to God. If you do your part to make your dreams come true, God will do His part. Instead of relying on God to make your dreams come true, you ought to be doing everything with your God-given skills, talents and resources you possibly can, knowing that God is supporting you along the way.

So instead of setting long-term goals with time spans that no one could possibly control, simply create your Monthly Method of Action and get to work. What could you accomplish this month if you really gave it your all?

Chances are, you can do a lot more than you've ever done before. We all have more potential inside us than we're used to using. I'm asking you to unleash your potential by setting higher expectations for yourself backed with a solid plan to get where you want to go.

CREATING YOUR ANNUAL METHOD OF ACHIEVEMENT (AMA)

Now that you've got your DMO and MMA, it's time to create your AMA. If it seems like we're doing things backwards, that's because *action* is more important than *talking about action.* The reason millions of people buy books on goal-setting every year and never accomplish their goals is because there's not enough action to back up those goals. Now that we've got your daily and monthly activity in place, it's time to create a plan for the year that will support you in doing *the right activities that lead to success.*

Your Annual Method of Achievement (AMA) is your long-term planning. It's where you look into the future and answer this question:

What opportunities can I take advantage of this year that will support me in achieving my goal?

Notice that we're not talking about goal-setting here. We're talking about *actions* that will help you take advantage of opportunities that will lead to your success (goal achievement).

Every year I look into the future and plan my AMA.

Here are the things I consider:

- ❖ What skills do I need to learn this year to grow my business?
- ❖ What books can I read this year that will help me achieve my goals?
- ❖ What seminars, workshops or courses can I attend this year that will help me achieve my goals?
- ❖ What groups or organizations can I join this year that will help me achieve my goals?
- ❖ Who could I meet or work with this year that will help me achieve my goals?

Notice that all of these questions aren't about *what* you're going to accomplish; they are about *how* you're going to accomplish your goals. We started this book with *why* so that you can live your life on purpose and become a highly paid author for the right reasons. Right now, we're talking about *how* you're going to accomplish your goals and live the life of your dreams.

Instead of focusing only on what you want, we're focusing on why you want what you want and how you're going to get it. And to do that, you must plan for the future. Many of the key opportunities that will change your life forever must be planned for. Reading the right books, attending the right seminars, writer's groups, writer's conferences, workshops and networking events—all of these activities must be planned ahead. Sure, you can wait for a friend to buy you a ticket to the next writer's conference or a stranger to give you a tip about the next book that will change your life, but why leave it up to chance? What if your friends don't come through? What if that stranger never shows up? Most people spend their entire lives waiting for other people to help them out. Instead, you ought to do whatever you can to help yourself! And by helping yourself, you'll be in a position to give back and help others at a much higher level than you ever could before. That's leadership.

A NOTE ABOUT WORK-LIFE BALANCE

Work-life balance has become a huge buzzword today touted as the "ultimate goal of life" for professionals in modern times. Personally, when I hear that phrase I want to puke. I believe work-life balance is a myth and is a completely inaccurate way to look at life. Proponents of this myth believe that there is a "perfect balance" that you can achieve by balancing "life" and "work" such that this perfect balance creates more happiness and fulfillment. Although I admire the intended outcomes, work-life balance is still a complete myth and anyone who tries to attain it will find themselves continually failing to achieve this coveted goal of perfect lifestyle design. Furthermore, anyone who believes that "life" is separate from "work" is completely delusional. *There is no difference between your life outside of work and your work. Your life is your work and your work is your life.* People who try do live "life" and "work" separately end up leading double-lives and find themselves always unfulfilled and disillusioned.

The truth is that *every single day of your life is different.* That's why your DMO isn't the only thing required for your success. You have to create a daily plan that takes into account new information, ideas and opportunities and you have to put that plan into action. Work-life balance proponents believe you can perfectly balance your life, proposing that maybe your ideal ratio should be 25% work, 25% family, 25% spiritual, and 25% blissful happiness.

I don't know about you, but I've never had a day that was *perfectly balanced.* I've had some days that were 90% work and other days that were 0% work. I've had some days that were 90% family time and other days that were 0% family time. I've had some days that were 90% dealing with other people's mistakes and so on. Every single day is different, and it's your days that make up your life. We all live just one day at a time. Instead of trying to strike the perfect work-life balance, just try to make today the best day you can.

Your actions today are the only thing you can control.

NASA can send a space ship to the moon and time the landing within a fraction of a second, but the shuttle will be off course 99% of the time! They have to constantly make adjustments to ensure the proper landing, but the landing is always proper. Likewise, you will be "out of balance" 99% of the time in your life, but you can still live the life of your dreams and achieve all your goals of becoming a highly successful author, having a loving family, and whatever else you want for your life. If you're a full-time author, you get to decide when to work and when to take time off.

Some days you will work far more than 8 hours and other times you may take the entire day off. If you do too much of one or the other, you'll burn out or go broke! In my personal experience, most people are willing to take far more days off than they are willing to work 16 hours a day and so the big opportunities to achieve their dreams fly right on by.

Personally, I love my work and I love what I do. The last time I worked a 16-hour day, I had an incredible day. I thoroughly enjoyed myself. To others, that may seem like a failure, but to me it feels like success, just as it does when I spend the entire day at the beach with my fiancé while others are working.

If you want to live the life of your dreams, you just have to accept that fact that you're going to be perpetually "out of balance" according to what other people think is the ideal work-life balance. If you want to be wildly successful in life, some days you'll have to work far more than others would say is appropriate, and other days you won't work even for a minute while others are slaving away in a job they can't stand. Is that work-life balance? I don't know, but it's the life that's led me to becoming a six-figure author, and it's the only life I can imagine that is worth living for me.

If you want my advice, forget about work-life balance. Focus on living the life of your dreams. *If there's a better life you dream about, what could be more "balanced" than living that life?* And if it takes some days where you work more than others, who cares? If that's the life you want to live, go for it! You don't have to conform to society's expectations of what a good life should look like. *This is your life! Live it the way **you** want.*

CHAPTER 8
BUILDING YOUR SUCCESS TEAM

WHY DO OVER 85% OF businesses fail in the first five years? Many say it's because of a lack of financing. Others say it's because of a lack of a business plan. I've been known to say it's because of a lack of marketing (which is true much of the time).

But the real underlying truth is that most businesses fail because they lack a successful team. If the team was the right team, they would be doing the right marketing and create the right business plan. I know it sounds cliché, but everything great that has ever been achieved has been achieved through teamwork. If you look at the Great Pyramids, or great companies like Apple, or man's first trip to the moon, or any truly great thing achieved by humans, they all required successful teams to make it happen.

Even if you look at geniuses like Isaac Newton or Albert Einstein, they didn't achieve their breakthroughs in science solely with their mind as most people think. Isaac Newton himself said, "If I see farther than the men before me, it's only because I stand on the shoulders of giants." We're all standing on the shoulders of giants—and if we don't see a little farther than those before us, it's only for a lack of vision, a lack of effort and a lack of initiative.

"No man is an island" is a famous quote that you have probably heard before. Yet so few authors, freelancers and small business owners apply this principle to their lives. And that's why they're not successful. Many freelancers, authors and business owners who work from home don't like to work with teams. Often, the reason is because of bad previous experiences with teams.

I remember in business school, our professors would assign us teams randomly and we would have to work with our "teammates" to create a report or a presentation on which we would all share a grade. The problem with these "teams" is that they serve no real purpose for the team even existing. Each of us on these teams could have created our own report or presentation in less time, with less effort and struggle if we simply worked on our own.

This is because tasks like creating a presentation or a report aren't very complex, and because working with others takes a lot of time and energy upfront to produce good results. In situations like this, working on a team is worse than working alone!

In the real world, teams don't work the way they do in school. In the real world, projects are much more complex and require very different skill sets and knowledge. If you write a book, you're going to need someone to edit it for you. That's teamwork right there. Whether you hire a professional editor or have your mom proofread it for you doesn't really matter—it's all teamwork.

But the heart of teamwork isn't "working together" as most corporate HR departments describe it. The heart of teamwork is each person doing their specialized task efficiently and effectively. It's about trust first and foremost. If you write a book, you have to trust that your editor is going to do a good job at editing it. And they have to trust that you're going to write a good book. No editor wants to edit a horrible book, and no writer wants a horrible editor.

> ***Successful people want to work with the best teammates they can find.***

It's a universal principle.

On the other hand, unsuccessful people don't want to work with the best teammates. They may feel threatened or insecure around successful people who perform at a high level. For whatever reason, unsuccessful people are unwilling or unable to create and maintain highly successful teams. In the wonderful book *Topgrading*, the authors talk about the importance of hiring A players for your business team. A players are successful people. This entire book is really just a blueprint for authors and writers who want to become A players or who are already A players and simply want to improve their skills even further. That's you!

Just remember no man or woman is an island. Even if you're the best A player writer in the world, you won't achieve any great success by yourself. You need a team to achieve great things in life! And your team MUST be filled with other A players if you hope to achieve the success you desire.

THE 7 TASKS OF HIGHLY SUCCESSFUL AUTHORS

Before we discuss how to create your A team, let's talk about what your team needs to do and accomplish first and foremost. These are the 7 key tasks that must get done so that you can become a highly paid author:

* Writing
* Editing
* Marketing
* Publishing
* Administrative Work
* Financial Management
* Technology / Web Work

Each of these areas can be broken down into subtasks or individual processes.

WRITING PROCESSES

* Brainstorming book ideas

- ❖ Outlining a book
- ❖ Character development (fiction)
- ❖ World development (fiction)
- ❖ Research
- ❖ Creative writing
- ❖ Transcribing (for authors who prefer to speak rather than write)

EDITING PROCESSES

- ❖ Proofreading
- ❖ Structural Editing
- ❖ Fact Checking
- ❖ Gathering Beta Reader Feedback

MARKETING PROCESSES

- ❖ Choosing a Book Title
- ❖ Cover Design
- ❖ Social Media
- ❖ Public Relations (PR)
- ❖ Guest Blogging

PRICING

- ❖ Promotions
- ❖ Advertising
- ❖ Writing Marketing and Sales Copy
- ❖ Distribution
- ❖ Search Engine Optimization (SEO)
- ❖ Publishing

COVER DESIGN

- ❖ Uploading Book Files

- ❖ Writing Book Descriptions
- ❖ Protecting Copyrights
- ❖ Collecting Royalties
- ❖ Managing Distribution Channels
- ❖ Managing Legal Issues
- ❖ Negotiating for Foreign Rights, Movie Rights and Subsidiary Rights

ADMINISTRATIVE WORK

- ❖ Checking Emails
- ❖ Answering Emails from Readers
- ❖ Compiling Royalty Reports and Sales Data
- ❖ Managing Social Media, Blogs, Reviews, and other feedback from readers

FINANCIAL MANAGEMENT

- ❖ Bookkeeping
- ❖ Compiling Royalty Reports and Sales Data
- ❖ Analyzing Royalty Reports and Sales Data
- ❖ Managing Cash Flow
- ❖ Paying Bills
- ❖ Filing and Paying Taxes

TECHNOLOGY / WEB WORK

- ❖ Creating a Website/Blog
- ❖ Managing a Website/Blog
- ❖ Creating Apps

HOW TO USE THESE LISTS

These lists of processes are not meant to be comprehensive. They're meant to give you an idea of the various tasks that go into creating a highly paid author business. Hopefully you will now see why it's so important to create a team to help you do all of that work.

The truth is that there is only one thing you need to do to become a highly paid author—write books. And even that can be delegated to a ghostwriter. So what you're really doing here is creating a team to help you achieve the results you want—becoming a highly paid author.

Whether you write your own books or hire a ghostwriter doesn't matter. Whether you do your own PR or hire a PR firm doesn't matter. What matters is that you create your own team and your own system that will make sure every key task necessary for your success is being done the right way for you.

I know some authors who are great web designers and they design their own websites. Yet I've read several books that say authors should never create their own website. "You MUST hire someone to create your author website for you!" shout the gurus. But that's not true for everyone. It doesn't matter who does the work as long as the work gets done and gets done well.

If you're a great web designer, then by all means create your own website. If you're a great accountant, then by all means manage your finances and taxes yourself. If you're a great graphic artist, then go ahead and design your book covers yourself. But if you're not great at these tasks, then you better find a good team member to help you out! Otherwise, the work won't get done or you'll do it so poorly that you'll have no hope of creating long-term success.

Creating an A team is all about understanding strengths and weaknesses. First of all, you must understand your own strengths and weaknesses. You must focus on activities that use your strengths. Then you must either improve your weaknesses to accomplish tasks well or find A players to take care of those tasks for you. That's leadership.

Leadership starts with you. That's why so far we've covered what YOU must do on a daily basis to succeed. We've talked about obstacles that

YOU must overcome to succeed. In short, we've talked about how to make you a better person. Now, you must apply these same principles to creating a better team.

YOUR REAL JOB AS AN AUTHOR

The real job you have to perform well to become a highly paid author isn't really a writing job at all! Of course, writing is a huge part of it, but it's just that—one part of many pieces to the puzzle. Your job is to make sure that all 7 key tasks get done. It doesn't really matter who does what as long as it gets done correctly. Do you understand now why most authors never sell more than a handful of books? It's because they focus just on writing and not much else gets done!

You must see yourself as running a bestselling author business, and not as simply a writer. Most authors, if they get lucky, find a publisher and then expect the publisher to take care of everything else except the writing. But you shouldn't do that.

Traditional publishers only focus on editing and publishing, and very rarely focus on marketing, except for their top clients who bring in all the profit. So you've still got 5 other key areas you must work on even if you have a traditional publisher—that's 5 times as much work as simply writing a book!

Just by knowing that there are 7 areas of authorship that you need to learn and be responsible for, you're light-years ahead of most other authors. Your real job as a highly paid author is to become a leader of your team. Your team will create bestselling books—not you!

Sure, you may be the author and write the book, and that's the most important part. But it's not enough by itself. We need others to help us succeed. We can't sit away locked in our room and write books and expect that anyone outside that room will ever care if we don't do the marketing, publishing and other necessary work that allows us to attract happy readers.

Instead, you must proactively build a team who will help you get your book edited, published and marketed professionally. I know many authors think they can do it all by themselves, and the truth is you can—but at what cost?

When you write the book all by yourself and you edit it all by yourself and you create the cover design by yourself and you build your own website and you self-publish your book and you do your own marketing... are you really creating a great product? Are you really doing an A job in each of those areas? Or are you an A writer, a B editor, a C cover designer and a D marketer?

Chances are, you're the latter. And if you try to do it all yourself, you will inevitably fail because you're competing against highly paid authors with A or B teams.

> *Even a B book with a B team will outsell an A book with no team!*

That's why the quickest and easiest route to selling more books is creating an A team. It takes a long time to become a better writer, but it doesn't take very long to build a team of good people to help you get your book edited, published and marketed well. You might not build a full A team right off the bat, but as long as each of your team members does a better job on their assigned task than you would, you've improved your chances of success, and you'll have more time to focus on writing. It takes time to build a great team, just like it takes time to achieve anything great in life. So be patient and focus on one step at a time.

Building a team isn't just a different way to look at authorship, it's an entirely different way of doing business. Authoring books is a business, and you can't master every area of this business all by yourself. Every pro in the industry knows this. That's why when you start building a team, you'll set yourself apart from all the solo-writers who think they are the best writer in the world and therefore deserve huge publishing deals for no reason other than the quality of their writing. How ridiculous! That's like the burger shop across the street from McDonald's going to a bank and requesting a loan bigger than the one McDonald's got because the burger shop makes better burgers. No one cares how good your burgers are if you don't have the team to run the business properly! I'm pretty sure a monkey could prepare a better burger than McDonald's does, but I don't know anyone who can run a business better than Ray Kroc did.

Instead of approaching agents and saying, "I have a great book, you should work with me," you should instead be saying, "I have a great team, and I think you might be a good fit. Let's talk and see if you would be a good asset for the team."

I know, it sounds silly. I know, it's not what other authors are saying. And that's exactly why you will stand out! Agents and publishers are tired of listening to solo-writers who think their writing alone qualifies them for some kind of special treatment or attention. They're looking for authors who understand that publishing is a team sport and that every area of the business must be performed well, not just the writing component.

When you start to build a team around you to help you master these 7 tasks of highly paid authors, you'll go from being a broke writer to a very successful author.

The key is to build your team and focus on the entire business of authorship instead of only focusing on the one task of writing.

RECRUITING YOUR TEAM

You must be absolutely persistent in recruiting *the right people* for your team. Remember, you're building an A-Team here and not a team of hobbyists. Finding A players is difficult. It takes time, effort and focus. Invest the time in recruiting the right teammates. That investment will pay huge dividends.

TIPS FOR RECRUITING TEAM MEMBERS

Always get at least three quotes from every contractor and interview at least three candidates for any job, position or contract. This protects you from making a poor hasty decision when there are better alternatives out there.

In addition, I highly recommend only hiring or recruiting people who are passionate about what they do. If they don't wake up in the morning excited about editing books, don't hire them as an editor! Because if they're not excited about what they're doing, you're going to have to motivate them to do it, which is a huge waste of your time and resources. And even when they do it, they won't do it as well as someone who's really excited and interested in that kind of work.

Work with people who are inspired if you want to live an inspired life.

CREATING CHECKLISTS

If you want to build a successful team, start falling in love with checklists. Every checklist you create is like having a new team member. Each checklist will save you hours of time, hassle and mistakes later on.

Every single commercial airline pilot in the world uses a checklist for every flight. Items on the checklist include basics like "turn the plane on" and "check fuel levels." Every item is so obvious, why even bother with a checklist? Because checklists save lives! In fact, the checklist is probably the greatest innovation in commercial airline safety that's ever been invented. Because the biggest cause of death in the industry is human error. And checklists prevent human error. That's why you need checklists for your business—to prevent human errors.

You should have a checklist for writing your book. You should have checklists for editing your books. You should have checklists for marketing, and checklists for cover design. You don't need to create your checklists right away. But you will create them over time as you learn more about what works for you and what doesn't work for you.

At first, when you're the only one on your team, using checklists might be silly. But it will save you a lot of time! Even us authors make mistakes, and having a checklist will prevent many of them. But even more importantly, having a checklist will allow you to simply hand the checklist to your new team members when you're ready to start delegating important tasks like editing and marketing. Without the checklist, you're just abdicating responsibility to your team. And that's not what leaders do. Leaders show people the way, and a checklist is an easy way to do that without getting bogged down in long meetings or back-and-forth emails over minutiae.

Here's what I recommend: every time you make a mistake, write it down. Then, add an item to your checklist that makes sure that mistake never happens again. Every time you do something that works really, really well, add an item to our checklist that ensures the next time around you repeat the necessary actions to make that happen.

Here's an example: let's say you're editing your novel and you realize that you mixed up the names of characters here and there throughout the book. A simple mistake, but one that's hard to catch if you're not really paying attention. Simply add an item to your "Editing Checklist" that says "check all character names and make sure they're used and spelled properly and consistently throughout."

I know, it sounds obvious and too simplistic. "Doesn't everyone already check for that?" you might think. But *if it's a mistake you made once before, you're guaranteed to do it again unless you change something*! That's what checklists are for—they help you prevent mistakes. Preventing mistakes saves you time and money and a lot of heartache.

Checklists also help you keep track of all the details and little things so that you can focus on the big things. If you're constantly worried about whether the character names are spelled right or whether the 12 crucial steps of your marketing plan were done correctly, you'll be too busy sweating the little stuff to focus on the important things that will move your business forward.

When you start using checklists, all the little things will be handled automatically; the checklists ensure that all those little things get done. So now you can focus on what's really, really important: writing and selling more books!

YOU ARE THE LEADER OF YOUR TEAM

You are the leader of your team! No one cares about your success as much as you do.

> *So if you don't get up early and stay up late to write your book, who will?*
>
> *If you're not marketing your books, who will?*
>
> *If you're not learning how to earn more money, who else will do that for you?*
>
> *If you're not absolutely committed to your own success, who else will be?*
>
> *No one!*

Your editors, publishers, agents, graphic designers, web designers, assistants, spouse's, kids, family, friends, colleagues, and peers don't care about your success like you do! They don't wake up in the morning thinking how they can make you be more successful. They wake up thinking about themselves.

If you want to create a successful team, you have to be so excited, so passionate, so inspired about your vision and creating the success you want that your team gets inspired by your vision. They have to see their own success intertwined with yours so that when they wake up in the morning thinking about how they can become even more successful, their goals and dreams are aligned with yours.

That's what leadership is really about. The only way you can achieve your goals as a leader is by helping your team achieve their goals. And when you do that, everyone wins. You win, your team wins, and your readers and customers win.

LEADERSHIP

Team members may come and go, but leaders stay for the long haul. Leadership is a rare quality and that's what makes you so valuable to your team. Your team needs you to lead them to success.

As a highly paid author, you're not just creating a great lifestyle for yourself, you're creating careers and stable incomes for your team. They depend on your success even more than you depend on them for yours.

If someone leaves your team, don't sweat it. You're a leader, and you can rebuild the team. Trust me, there are plenty more editors, web designers, graphic designers, agents, etc. out there. But you are the leader, and you can't be replaced. You have to lead on ~~even~~ especially when times get tough.

CHAPTER 9
CREATING LONG-TERM SUCCESS

NOW THAT YOU'VE LEARNED THE 7 crucial tasks of becoming a highly paid author, how to create your DMO for success, how to build your success team, and how to grow your business as an author, it's time to start planning ahead for your long-term success.

You know now that becoming a highly paid author isn't about getting rich quick or overnight success. It's not about one little magic bullet or strategy that's guaranteed to make you rich. Becoming successful requires that you focus on what's important and do what's necessary to write and sell more books.

Don't be like the millions of other authors out there who think short-term. The ones who write a book, self-publish it without editing, don't do any marketing, and then cross their fingers and hope to win the lottery. Now, there's nothing wrong or bad about doing things this way. It just won't lead you to the success you want!

If you truly want to become a highly paid author, then you must start focusing on long-term success and not short-term results.

Instead of focusing on how many books you sold this week, focus on what you did this week that will help you sell more books in the long-term. Did you write some new material this week? Did you market and promote your books? Did you take some actions to build your A team? What did you do that will have a positive, long-term effect on your success? That's what you must focus on!

I've said for years that long-term success in life and in business require long-term relationships. You must be focused on creating long-term relationships with yourself as a writer, with your readers, and your team members. I've seen new writers spend a year writing a book, publish it, and then when sales weren't what they expected, they quit! They stop writing and go back to find another get-rich-quick scheme. Instead of running around in circles chasing new opportunities, commit yourself to becoming a successful author.

> *The biggest mistake you can ever make in life is giving up on your dreams.*

Who cares if it takes 1 year or 10 years or 50 years to achieve your dream? It's better to live your dream than to settle for something that's not important to you. If writing is really important to you, don't give up! Never, ever, ever give up!

I know, the path isn't covered with chocolates and candy rainbows. I know, it's going to be difficult. I know, you're going to feel like giving up sometimes.

I know what it feels like because I've been there! I know what it's like to struggle for six years not knowing how to get my book published. I know what it's like to publish my book and sell less than 10 copies a month. I know what it's like to have a little bit of success, and then publish a new book thinking it will do well and see it flop. I know what it's like to get 1-star reviews and have readers tear my book apart. I know what it's like to have family and friends think I'm an idiot for writing. I know what it's like to be plagiarized, to have others steal my work and claim it as their own. To have others blatantly violate my copyrights and sell entire books I wrote for their profit. I know what it's like to wake up at 4am and wonder if it's even worth it to get out of bed and start writing.

Trust me, whatever challenges, struggles or setbacks you face along the way, someone else has already faced and overcome those challenges! If they can do it, you can do it.

But, the truth is, I'm glad I know all these things. I'm glad I know how horrible it feels to not sell any books, and I'm glad for all the negative, painful and heartbreaking experiences I've had along the way. I'm glad because I know that without those painful experiences, I wouldn't be where I am today. I wouldn't be living my dream.

If writing is your dream, then I wish you many painful experiences along the way so that you too can be proud of your accomplishments and know that your journey to becoming a highly paid author was well worth the price you paid. I hope this book has inspired you to follow your dreams and to never give up.

Here's to your success!

THE KINDLE BIBLE SERIES

I F YOU LIKED THIS BOOK then you will love reading my books in the Kindle Bible Series.

The Kindle Writing Bible is the first book in the series which covers in detail how to come up with bestselling nonfiction books ideas and turn them into a reality using cutting edge writing productivity strategies, tools and resources.

The Kindle Formatting Bible is the next step in the process. It takes you through step-by-step formatting tutorials to show you how to format your book for Kindle using Microsoft Word. It also walks you through the process of uploading your book to Kindle.

The Kindle Publishing Bible is the next book in the series. It's all about the marketing! The book shows you how to choose bestselling book titles and provides a step-by-step marketing system that anyone can use to sell a lot more books quickly.

The Amazon Analytics Bible is the final book in the series which goes into even more detail about how to use analytics to sell more books. In this book, I also share detailed statistics from my own personal KDP Select free promotions and show you why you MUST be in KDP Select unless you can easily get over 100 targeted visitors to your book sales pages every single day (that's over 3,000 a month!).

Kindle Success Stories is a recent addition to the series. In this book, I researched the top self-published Kindle authors in the world and asked them to share their stories, lessons and tips for new and aspiring authors. Many of these authors have sold hundreds of thousands of Kindle eBooks, and some of them have sold millions.

SPECIAL FACEBOOK GROUP

COME JOIN OUR FACEBOOK GROUP just for readers like you who want to take their marketing to the next level. In this group we share our successes, marketing tips and strategies with each other so that we can all continue to grow our businesses together.

This is also a fantastic group for finding joint venture partners and cross-promotion opportunities! Imagine if you had hundreds of other entrepreneurs from all over the world collaborating with you—think how big of an impact you could have.

It's also a great place to get any marketing questions you have answered as well.

Come join us on Facebook:

www.facebook.com/groups/KindlePublishers

FREE BLOGGING FOR BUSINESS TRAINING

IF YOU'RE A BUSINESS OWNER and want to learn how to start a blog for your business that makes a profit, I've developed a free online training program to teach you everything from how to build your blog to getting traffic to monetizing it.

You can get the free training at:

www.BlogBusinessSchool.com

FREE TWITTER TRAINING

TO THANK YOU FOR BUYING this book I want to give you my best-selling book on How To Make Money With Twitter as a special bonus.

I've been using Twitter for years to get hundreds of new leads a month for my online businesses and it's a great way to promote your books in very little time once you set the system up.

You can grab your free copy at:

www.blogbusinessschool.com/how-to-make-money-with-twitter

WANT TO GET PUBLISHED?

I F YOU'VE WRITTEN ONE OR several books and just want to focus on your writing, you might want to consider publishing with TCK Publishing founded by Tom Corson-Knowles. We'll help you choose the right title and help with market research ahead of time so your book will sell better. We also do all the formatting for Kindle, cover design, publishing and a lot of marketing for our clients.

Many of our clients have already become bestselling authors. Will you be next?

We publish both nonfiction and fiction books. Learn more at:

www.tckpublishing.com/publish-your-book-with-us

CONNECT WITH TOM

THANK YOU SO MUCH FOR taking the time to read this book. I'm excited for you to start your path to creating the life of your dreams as a Kindle author.

If you have any questions of any kind, feel free to contact me directly via email at: *Tom@TCKPublishing.com*

You can follow me on Twitter: *@JuiceTom*

And connect with me on Facebook:
www.Facebook.com/tomcorsonknowles

You can check out my publishing blog for the latest updates here:
www.TCKpublishing.com

I'm wishing you the best of health, happiness and success!

Here's to you!

Tom Corson-Knowles

ABOUT THE AUTHOR

TOM CORSON-KNOWLES is the #1 Amazon best-selling author of *The Kindle Publishing Bible* and *How To Make Money With Twitter*, among others. He lives in Kapaa, Hawaii. Tom loves educating and inspiring other entrepreneurs to succeed and live their dreams.

Learn more at: *www.Amazon.com/Author/Business*

OTHER BOOKS BY TOM CORSON-KNOWLES

Systemize, Automate, Delegate: How to Grow a Business While Traveling, on Vacation and Taking Time Off

The Kindle Publishing Bible: How To Sell More Kindle eBooks On Amazon

The Kindle Writing Bible: How To Write a Bestselling Nonfiction Book From Start To Finish

The Kindle Formatting Bible: How To Format Your Ebook For Kindle Using Microsoft Word

The Amazon Analytics Bible: How To Use Analytics To Sell More Books

How To Make Money With Twitter

The Blog Business Book: How To Start A Blog And Turn It Into A Six Figure Online Business

Facebook For Business Owners: Facebook Marketing For Fan Page Owners and Small Businesses

Rich by 22: How To Achieve Business Success at an Early Age

How To Reduce Your Debt Overnight: A Simple System To Eliminate Credit Card And Consumer Debt

The Network Marketing Manual: Work From Home And Get Rich In Direct Sales

101 Ways To Start A Business For Less Than $1,000

ONE LAST THING...

THANKS FOR READING! IF YOU enjoyed this book or found it useful I'd be very grateful if you'd post a short review on Amazon. Your support really does make a difference and I read all the reviews personally so I can get your feedback and make this book even better.

If you'd like to leave a review then all you need to do is click the review link on this book's page on Amazon at:

www.amzn.to/16xo4QX

Thanks again for your support!

Made in the USA
Charleston, SC
01 February 2014